The Early Modern Englishwoman:
A Facsimile Library of Essential Works

Series II

Printed Writings, 1641–1700: Part 1

Volume 3

Mother's Advice Books

Selected and Introduced by
Susan C. Staub

General Editors
Betty S. Travitsky and Patrick Cullen

Ashgate

Aldershot • Burlington USA • Singapore • Sydney

Published by
Ashgate Publishing Limited
Gower House
Croft Road
Aldershot
Hants GU11 3HR
England

Ashgate Publishing Company
131 Main Street
Burlington, VT 05401–5600 USA

Ashgate website: http://www.ashgate.com

British Library Cataloguing-in-Publication Data
The early modern Englishwoman : a facsimile library of
    essential works
    Part 1: Printed writings, 1641–1700 : Vol. 3: Mother's
    advice books
    1. English literature – Early modern, 1500–1700   2. English
    literature – Women authors   3. Women – England – History –
    Renaissance, 1450–1600 – Sources   4. Women – England –
    History – Modern period, 1600 – – Sources   5. Women – Literary
    collections
    I. Staub, Susan C.   II. Travitsky, Betty S.   III. Cullen,
    Patrick
    820.8'09287

Library of Congress Cataloging-in-Publication Data
The early modern Englishwoman: a facsimile library of essential works. Part 1. Printed
Writings 1641–1700 / general editors, Betty S. Travitsky and Patrick Cullen.

See page vi for complete CIP Block 00–64296

The image reproduced on the title page and on the case is taken from the frontispiece portrait in *Poems. By the Most Deservedly Admired Mrs. Katherine Philips* (1667). Reproduced by permission of the Folger Shakespeare Library, Washington, DC.

ISBN 0 7546 0210 9

Printed in Great Britain by Antony Rowe Ltd, Chippenham, Wiltshire

The Early Modern Englishwoman:
A Facsimile Library of Essential Works

Series II

Printed Writings, 1641–1700: Part 1

Volume 3

Mother's Advice Books

CONTENTS

Library of Congress Cataloging-in-Publication Data

Mother's advice books / selected and introduced by Susan C. Staub.

     p. cm. – (The early modern Englishwoman. Printed writings, 1641–1700, Part 1; v. 3)
     Includes bibliographical references.

     Contents: A ladies legacie to her davghters / by Madam Elizabeth Richardson – The legacy of a dying mother to her mourning children / Mrs. Susanna Bell – The mother's blessing – Dear children, harken diligently to the counsel and advice of your parents, for they watch over you for your good / Mary Pennyman, Appendix from John Pennyman's instructions to his children – Containing some few of the directions she wrote for her children's instruction..., Appendix from Anthony Walker's The holy life of Mrs. Elizabeth Walker.

    ISBN 0 7546 0210 9

     1. Christian women–Conduct of life–Early works to 1800. 2. Women–England–History–17th century–Sources. I. Cramond, Elizabeth Richardson, Baroness, d. 1651. Ladies legacie to her davghters. II. Bell, Susanna, d. 1672. Legacy of a dying mother to her mourning children. III. Pennyman, John, 1628–1706. John Pennyman's instructions to his children. Selections. IV. Pennyman, Mary, 1630–1701. Dear children, harken diligently to the counsel and advice of your parents, for they watch over you for your good. V. Walker, Anthony, d. 1692. Holy life of Mrs. Elizabeth Walker. Selections VI. Walker, Elizabeth, 1623–1690. Containing some few of the directions she wrote for her children's instruction... VII. Staub, Susan C. VIII. Mother's blessing. IX. Title: Ladies legacie to her davghters. X. Title: Legacy of a dying mother to her mourning children. XI. Title: Dear children, harken diligently to the counsel and advice of your parents, for they watch over you for your good. XII. Title: Containing some few of the directions she wrote for her children's instruction... XIII. Series.

BJ1610 .M655 2000
170'.44'094209032--dc21

                                              00–64296

PREFACE
BY THE GENERAL EDITORS

Until very recently, scholars of the early modern period have assumed that there were no Judith Shakespeares in early modern England. Much of the energy of the current generation of scholars has been devoted to constructing a history of early modern England that takes into account what women actually wrote, what women actually read, and what women actually did. In so doing the masculinist representation of early modern women, both in their own time and ours, is deconstructed. The study of early modern women has thus become one of the most important—indeed perhaps the most important—means for the rewriting of early modern history.

The Early Modern Englishwoman: A Facsimile Library of Essential Works is one of the developments of this energetic reappraisal of the period. As the names on our advisory board and our list of editors testify, it has been the beneficiary of scholarship in the field, and we hope it will also be an essential part of that scholarship's continuing momentum.

The Early Modern Englishwoman is designed to make available a comprehensive and focused collection of writings in English from 1500 to 1750, both by women and for and about them. The three series of *Printed Writings* (1500–1640, 1641–1700, and 1701–1750) provide a comprehensive if not entirely complete collection of the separately published writings by women. In reprinting these writings we intend to remedy one of the major obstacles to the advancement of feminist criticism of the early modern period, namely the limited availability of the very texts upon which the field is based. The volumes in the facsimile library reproduce carefully chosen copies of these texts, incorporating significant variants (usually in appendices). Each text is preceded by a short introduction providing an overview of the life and work of a writer along with a survey of important scholarship. These works, we strongly believe, deserve a large readership—of historians, literary critics, feminist critics, and non-specialist readers.

The Early Modern Englishwoman also includes separate facsimile series of *Essential Works for the Study of Early Modern Women* and of *Manuscript Writings*. These facsimile series are complemented by *The Early Modern Englishwoman 1500–1750: Contemporary Editions*. Also under our general editorship, this series will include both old-spelling and modernized editions of works by and about women and gender in early modern England.

New York City
2001

INTRODUCTORY NOTE

The three texts included in this volume, Elizabeth Richardson's *A Ladies Legacie to her Davghters*, Susanna Bell's *The Legacy of a Dying Mother To Her Mourning Children*, and the unattributed *The Mothers Blessing: Being Several Godly Admonitions given by a Mother unto her Children upon her Death-bed* are variants of the category of works identified by Elaine Beilin as 'Mother's Advice Books'. One of the many sub-genres of courtesy literature, mother's advice books are texts written by mothers instructing their children in religious, educational, and occasionally, worldly matters. Although many advice books survive from the sixteenth and seventeenth centuries, most of these were written by men and were concerned with policy and polite conduct. Many men wrote books of advice specifically addressed to their children: Sir Walter Raleigh, *Instructions to his Sonne and to Posteritie (1632)*; Francis Osborne, *Advice to a Son (1656)*; and John Heyden, *Advice to a Daughter, In Opposition to the Advice to a Sonne (1658)* to name just a few. Mother's advice books, on the other hand, were more unusual. Written by women speaking from their authorized positions as mothers, they offer an alternative to the many male-authored conceptualizations of the family from the period. These texts are important because they provide an example of women writing within a socially sanctioned area. The fact that these women were mothers (as well as the fact that most of them died before publication of their works) gave them an authority to write that other women were not easily granted. While the act of writing itself might have been transgressive, their subject – the education of their children – was thoroughly traditional. But more importantly, although they feign a private voice, many of these works were clearly written with an eye towards publication. In a period that sought to limit female authority to the domestic sphere, it was precisely the domestic role of mother that allowed these women entrance into the public sphere represented by publication.

The mother's advice book, then, is a genre that at once violates and yet replicates patriarchal dictates.

The popularity of some mother's advice books such as that written by Dorothy Leigh suggests the increased authority of the mother and hints at the potential for increased female social power in the period. Leigh's *A Mother's Blessing*, first published in 1616, ran through at least a dozen editions before 1640 and was republished four times in the period covered by this volume: 1656 (Wing L980), 1663 (Wing L981), 1667 (Wing L981A) and 1674 (Wing L982). Elizabeth Joceline's *The Mothers legacie to her unborn child* was also republished during this period (1684, Wing J756).

There are several examples of mothers writing to their children during the period 1641–1700 and many more of these texts may be lost, such as Lady Anne Halkett's *Mother's Will to her Unborn Child*, written during her first pregnancy in 1656. Mothers, such as Lady Halkett and Lady Ann Fanshawe, also offered advice to their children in letters, autobiographies and memoirs. Still other women used their positions as mothers to publish their works and enter religious and political debates under the guise of advice to children. This was true of the prolific Lady Eleanor Davies (or Douglas), whose work *From the Lady Eleanor, Her Blessing to her beloved Daughter* (1644) is a critique of the civil war and an allegory on the British monarchy. Yet another variant of the genre appears in *A Fair Warning to Murderers of Infants*, a crime pamphlet from the period which includes a long letter, 'Advice of your Dying Mother', ostensibly dictated by a mother convicted of murdering one of her children. Whether actually dictated by the mother or not, the letter suggests that Dorothy Leigh and other writing mothers were influential enough for the pamphleteer to use them as models for his repentant mother.

Although the category of mother's advice book is a vague one and might include many kinds of writing, the texts included here are notable for their development of a motherly persona, their emphasis on spiritual and domestic matters and their characterization of the works as legacies. In addition to the three main texts, this volume also reprints portions of two predominantly male-authored texts that record a mother's instruction to her children: Mary Pennyman's letter to her children, published as part of *John Pennyman's Instructions to his Children*, and Elizabeth Walker's 'For my Dear Children, Mrs. Margaret and Elizabeth Walker', included in Anthony Walker's *The Holy Life of Mrs. Elizabeth Walker*.

Elizabeth Richardson

The daughter of Catherine and Sir Thomas Beaumont, Elizabeth Richardson was of the same family as Lady Villiers, mother of the Duke of Buckingham. Married twice, Elizabeth bore six children to her first husband, John Ashburnham. Left destitute after Ashburnham's death in 1620, Richardson (d. 1651) laments the fact that she cannot bequeath her daughters 'portions of Wealth', but hoping nonetheless to raise their 'portion of Grace'(4), she offers as a substitute a three-part collection of prayers and meditations entitled *A Ladies Legacie to her Davghters*. Richardson began the first book of her legacy in 1625 'when the great sicknesse was in London' (3). In 1626 she married Sir Thomas Richardson and in 1628 became Baroness of Cramond when her husband was prevented from holding the honour because of his position as a judge. When she was widowed again in 1634, Richardson continued her writing to her daughters, using the second book to grapple with her feelings of grief and loneliness. She wrote the third book after suffering 'a long and great fit of sicknesse' (165). All three books were published together in 1645, addressed now to her four daughters and to her sons' wives as a 'motherly remembrance' (5).

A Ladies Legacie to her Davghters

Initially, Richardson imagines an entirely female audience and excludes her sons, 'lest being men, they misconstrue my well-meaning; yet I presume that you my daughters will not refuse your Mothers teaching (which I wish may be your ornament and a crown of glory to you)' (6). But in an autographed letter in the front leaves of the Houghton Library (Harvard University) copy of the work, she presents it to her grandson hoping that he will 'p[ar]don & excuse, all defectes theirin, yt comes from me, a weake vnlearned woman'. In adopting the pose of a 'weake vnlearned woman' Richardson exhibits the same self-consciousness as other writing mothers and feels compelled to apologize for publishing her work. She admits that a woman's 'endeavour may be contemptible to many' but 'devotions or prayers', she contends, 'surely concernes and belongs to women, as well as to the best learned men' (3). Although she asserts that she intended her meditations for her own private use, and that of her children, she concedes that she was persuaded to make them public. The ruse of reluctance to publish was a standard convention for both male and female writers during the period, but the woman writer's apologia was crucial because writing women challenged the patriarchal insistence on female silence. Nonetheless, despite her apologies Richardson seems to have a sense of a more public readership. She includes a letter 'To the Reader' at the beginning of Book II that she addressed to parents in general, and both the Bodleian and Houghton copies of the text include careful authorial emendations throughout, because, she complains, 'it is so falsely printed'. While the text itself suggests a private maternal voice, the prefatory material and authorial changes show a writer thoroughly aware of her public voice.

The maternal persona Richardson creates is one of both authority and poignancy. At times stern and chastising, she reminds her daughters of the pain she endured in bringing them into the world and of her continued solicitude for the salvation of their souls. In that endeavour, Richardson brings together prayers and meditations for every occasion, including several that are extremely personal and private. Distinctly Protestant in their focus on scriptures, they also reflect her struggles as a mother and widow.

Wing notes four copies of *A Ladies Legacie to her Davghters* (1645), held by the British, Bodleian, Huntington and Houghton Libraries. Sylvia Brown includes *A Ladies Legacie* in her collection of mother's advice books entitled, *Women's Writing in Stuart England: The Mothers' Legacies of Dorothy Leigh, Elizabeth Joscelin and Elizabeth Richardson*. A portion of the text is also reprinted in Otten, *English Women's Voices, 1540–1700*. The British Library and Huntington copies provide examples of the text as originally published without authorial changes. The copy owned by the Bodleian was originally intended as a presentation copy to Richardson's brother and includes emendations by the author. The facsimile reproduced here is from the Houghton Library copy. Also a presentation book, this time to her grandson, Sir Edward Dering, this copy also includes authorial corrections throughout the text as well as a long letter to Dering written on the inside front cover and signed Eliz. Cramond. The binding bears Dering's initials. In this copy Richardson emends the title to read *A Mothers Legacie to her Sixe Daughters*.

Susanna Bell

Most of the facts we know about Susanna Bell (d. 1672) are those narrated by Bell herself in *The Legacy of a Dying Mother* or given by the Independent minister Thomas Brooks (1608–1680) in his prefatory letter to the work. Brought up in a religious and God-fearing family, Bell initially resisted when her husband sought to join the Puritan emigration to New England in the 1620s. After her refusal she suffered a miscarriage, bringing about a crisis of faith and prompting her to rethink her relationship with God and with her husband. She finally agreed to travel to New England, and she relates her experiences both there and after her return to England in this text, her deathbed remembrance of her life.

The Legacy of a Dying Mother

Published posthumously in 1673 under the sponsorship of Brooks, *The Legacy of a Dying Mother* is composed of two parts: Brooks' 'Epistle Dedicatory' (almost twice the length of Bell's portion) and Bell's narrative of her life, dictated to her son. Less explicit in its advice than other works of this genre, Bell uses her life experiences as a cautionary lesson for her four surviving children. As much a conversion tale as an advice book, *The Legacy of a Dying Mother* is as 'concerned with Bell's conversion to the merits of wifely duty' as it is 'with more mystical matters', according to Elaine Hobby (p. 71). Christine Sizemore argues, in fact, that *The Legacy of a Dying*

Mother does not constitute an advice book at all (1981, p. 67 n. 21). But it is included here because it follows the form in intent if not content; Bell's work is valuable as a variant of the genre. Bell's writing is also of historic significance, offering a firsthand account of a woman's experience in New England. With its focus on marriage and childbearing, as well as its references to the war in England, sermons by Mr. Cotton, the Great Fire and other topical events, it presents a vivid account of the domestic and spiritual concerns of a seventeenth-century Englishwoman in the colonies.

This text also differs from the other works included here because the characteristic justification for publication is written not by the mother herself but by Brooks in his prefatory letter. Although Brooks notes that Bell desired to have her narrative published, Brooks' voice overwhelms Bell's, and it is he who constructs her as the ideal of motherly affection and virtue. As Brooks creates the persona of their 'glorified Mother', he urges Bell's children to follow the instruction offered by her holy life. Bell's life itself becomes her advice book.

The Legacy of a Dying Mother was republished in *The Complete Works of Thomas Brooks*, ed. A. B. Grosart (1866). A portion of Bell's narrative is also included in *Lay by Your Needles Ladies, Take the Pen* (Trill, Chedgzoy and Osborne, eds). Of the three copies listed in Wing B1801 (misnumbered B1802 in the 1972 ed.), the one owned by the Boston Public Library was chosen for reproduction here because it is the most legible.

The Mothers Blessing

Although nothing is known of the anonymous writer of *The Mothers Blessing: Being Several Godly Admonitions given by a Mother unto her Children upon her Death-bed, a little before her departure*, the work seems clearly influenced by Dorothy Leigh and other writing mothers. From the title to the explanation for writing, the author follows the pattern established in earlier mother's advice books. In fact, the similarity of titles has often led to the false attribution of the text to Leigh. Claiming that her present sickness is 'deaths harbinger' and that she possesses little wealth to leave her children, the speaker offers them her writing as her legacy.

The book is composed of three main parts: a four-page prose introduction with the title 'An Hvndred Godly Lessons', a section in verse entitled 'An Hundred Devout Admonitions left by a Dying mother to her children', and the mother's concluding prayer, spoken even as she breathes her last breath. There is also an appended series of biblical maxims in a different typeface. After the prose introduction, which is largely religious in tone, the advice presented is more far-ranging and practical than in most mother's advice books, with few of the biblical references which characterize other works of this kind. The maternal persona is authoritative and sometimes sharp: 'if you shall slight my speeches, and tread these precepts underfoot, you shall neither be happy here, nor blest hereafter' (B2-B2v). The distinguishing feature of this text is its use of verse: 'because Songs and rhimes may make a better impression, and stick faster in your memories,' according to the mother (A4v). (Dorothy Leigh prefaces her treatise with a short section of verse, but the bulk of her book is in prose.) The use of verse links this work to earlier advice books, such as *The Northern Mother's Blessing*, M. R.'s *The Mothers Counsell, or Live within Compasse*, and Nicholas Breton's *The Mothers Blessing* (1602), in which Breton initially adopts the persona of a mother but acknowledges that he is the author of the piece.

The connection with Breton lends some weight to the conjecture that the present work may actually have been written by a man. Bell, Parfitt and Shepherd attribute *The Mothers Blessing* to a woman in *English Women Writers, 1580–1720* as does Patricia Crawford in her survey 'Women's Published Writings 1600–1700', but the hazy publication history of the text makes the position difficult to prove. If Sloan is correct in his assertion that the verse included in this text was published c. 1650 as the broadside ballad 'An Hundred Godly Lessons' (see Wing H 3726 and H3726A, dated 1670–97 and 1674–79, respectively) and reissued twenty-five years later in a more expanded form, the author may have written from the perspective of a mother in order to capitalize on the popularity of Leigh. What is certain is that the verse was popular enough to be reissued as a broadside well into the nineteenth century.

In his notes to *The Roxburghe Ballads* W. Chappell questions the attribution of 'An Hundred Godly Lessons' to a woman because he finds the tone sometimes 'neither charitable nor christian'. Citing a verse that he finds particularly troublesome because of its use of the word 'hate' ('Hate her that doth on every man/set her delights and joy'), Chappell concludes, however, that the author must be a woman since 'women are, proverbially, said to be more bitter on those subjects than men' (427). Despite his rather dated arguments, the tone and concerns of the opening prose section of the text are consistent with other mother's advice books, and most of the lessons of the ballad are the kind that could be given by a parent of either sex.

Wing includes one entry for *The Mothers Blessing* (M2937) and locates copies in the Thomason Collection of the British Library; Magdalene College, Cambridge; and the Bodleian Library. The Bodleian Library and Magdalene College copies (1685) are complete with title pages, but several pages in the Bodleian copy are in very poor condition. A unique version is housed in the Pierpont Morgan Library. Although the catalogue record dates this work 1665, there is no date in the text itself. This copy includes only the four-page prose section. The sales information from Sothebys mistakenly attributes the book to Leigh, noting, 'This early chapbook is apparently an extract or abridged version of Dorothy Leigh's *The Mother's Blessing*, first printed in 1616'. The British Library copy, reproduced here and chosen because it is the most legible copy, is conjecturally dated 1670, although the date is missing from the title page.

Appendix

Mary Pennyman

The daughter of the royalist Edmund Heron, Mary Pennyman was married twice, first to Henry Boremam, a Quaker with whom she had three children, and after Boremam's death, to John Pennyman. The marriage to Pennyman was considered scandalous by many Quakers, a religion Pennyman was rejecting by this point, and the wedding was lampooned in a ballad entitled 'Ye Quakers Wedding'. In addition to various letters and papers, Pennyman wrote a Quaker tract, *Something formerly writ foreseen and foretold* (1676), and with John Pennyman, *The Ark is Begun to be Opened* (1671).

'Dear Children ... '

Her brief letter to her children is included in *John Pennyman's Instructions to his Children*, a small pamphlet of fatherly advice first published in 1674. In it, Pennyman exhorts her children to heed their 'Fathers Counsel' and 'trust in the Lord only' (13). At least eight copies of this edition survive. Later editions appeared in 1681, 1684 and 1690 under the title *The Way to Peace and Happiness proposed in some Instructions, given formerly by a parent to his children* (Wing P1425–1427) and in 1697 as *Some Needful Instructions for Youth* (Wing P1415A). The present facsimile is based on the 1674 copy (Wing P1407) held by the Bodleian Library, Oxford and is used here because it is cut and bound in a way that allows reproduction.

Elizabeth Walker

The eldest daughter of John and Elizabeth Sadler, Elizabeth Walker was born in 1623 in London. In 1650 she married Anthony Walker. She bore eleven children in the course of her marriage, none of whom survived her. Walker was a prolific writer, turning out private texts such as memoirs, diary entries, meditations, prayers and letters, but she begged her husband to keep her papers private while she lived. Remaining true to his wife's wishes, Anthony Walker waited until after her death in 1690 to publish his lengthy biography of her, *The Holy Life of Mrs. Elizabeth Walker*. Although Anthony Walker drew heavily on Elizabeth's writings in his narration of her life, most of the biography is a third person summary with her words indicated in quotation marks. Elizabeth Walker's 'For my Dear Children, Mrs. Margaret and Elizabeth Walker' is appended to the biography.

'An Appendix ... '

Two editions of *The Holy Life of Mrs. Elizabeth Walker* were published in 1690 (Wing W305 and W305A); another version appeared in 1694 under the title *The Vertuous Wife; or, the Holy Life of Mrs. Elizabth* [sic] *Walker* (Wing W311A). In the selection reproduced here by permission of the Folger Shakespeare Library (Wing W305), Anthony Walker gives a brief explanation for including Elizabeth's instructions to her children and then allows her to speak in her own voice.

References

Wing R1382 [Richardson]; B1801 (numbered B1802 in 1972 ed.) [Bell]; M2937 [*The Mothers Blessing*]; P1407 [Pennyman]; W305 [Walker]

Beilin, Elaine (1987), *Redeeming Eve: Women Writers of the English Renaissance*, Princeton: Princeton University Press

Bell, Maureen, George Parfitt, and Simon Shepherd (1990), *A Biographical Dictionary of English Women Writers 1580–1720*, Boston: G.K. Hall & Co.

Blain, Virginia, Patricia Clements and Isobel Grundy (eds) (1990), *The Feminist Companion to Literature in English: Women Writers from the Middle Ages to the Present*, New Haven, CT: Yale University Press

Brown, Sylvia (1999), *Women's Writing in Stuart England: The Mothers' Legacies of Dorothy Leigh, Elizabeth Joscelin and Elizabeth Richardson*, Phoenix Hill: Sutton Publishing Limited

Crawford, Patricia (1991), 'Women's Published Writings 1600–1700' in Prior, Mary (ed.), *Women in English Society 1500–1800*, London and New York: Routledge

Feroli, Teresa (1994), '"Infelix Simulacrum": The Rewriting of Loss in Elizabeth Jocelin's The Mothers Legacie', *English Literary History* 61 (1): 89–102

Hobby, Elaine (1989), *Virtue of Necessity: English Women's Writing, 1649–88*, Ann Arbor: University of Michigan Press

Otten, Charlotte (1992), *English Women's Voices, 1540–1700*, Miami: Florida International University Press

Poole, Kristen (1995), '"The Fittest Closet for All Goodness": Authorial Strategies of Jacobean Mothers' Manuals', *Studies in English Literature* 35(1): 69–88

Rose, Mary Beth (1991), 'Where Are the Mothers in Shakespeare? Options for Gender Representation in the English Renaissance', *Shakespeare Quarterly* 42 (3): 291–314

The Roxburghe Ballads (1966), Volume 1, with notes by W. Chappell, New York: AMS Press, Inc.

Sizemore, Christine W. (1976), 'Early Seventeenth-Century Advice Books: The Female Viewpoint', *South Atlantic Bulletin* 41 (1): 41–48

— (1981), 'Attitudes Toward the Education and Roles of Women: Sixteenth-Century Humanists and Seventeenth-Century Advice Books', *University of Dayton Review* 15 (1): 57–67

Sloane, William (1955), *Children's Books in England and America in the Seventeenth Century*, New York: King's Crown Press

Travitsky, Betty S. (1980), 'The New Mother of the English Renaissance: Her Writings on Motherhood' in Davidson, Cathy and Broner, E. M. (eds), *The Lost Tradition: Mothers and Daughters in Literature*, New York: Ungar

Trill, Suzanne, Kate Chedgzoy and Melanie Osborne (eds) (1997), *Lay by Your Needles Ladies, Take the Pen: Women Writing in England, 1500–1700*, London: Arnold

Wayne, Valerie (1996), 'Advice for Women from Mothers and Patriarchs' in Wilcox, Helen (ed.), *Women and Literature in Britain 1500–1700*, New York: Cambridge University Press

SUSAN C. STAUB

Elizabeth Richardson, *A Ladies Legacie to her Davghters* (Wing R1382) is reproduced by permission of the Houghton Library, Harvard University. The text block measures 75×120 mm, sig. A3.

The text contains the following misnumberings. (The correct number appears in brackets.):

p. 161 [162], p. 162 [163]

Readings where the copy is torn or blurred:

The last three lines of page 17:
keep the same, with a conscionable care to practise what I shall learne thereby, devoutly calling
upon thy most holy Name, and using due reverence

The last three lines of page 18:
thy righteousnesse; that so all thy graces may daily
increase in me, and my humble and unperfect service in calling on thy holy name, may grow daily

The last two lines of page 47:
thee for helpe: yet beyond all hope, thou didst
bring them back from the gates of death, praised

This, for my dearly beloued & worthy
Grandson, Ed: Dering K: Baronet

My sonne-worthy, & first Grand-Child, I psent
(as due) this poore Booke vnto you, wch at
first Intended, only for all my Children &
Grand-children; for their Instruction in
ye youth, & for their vse, & remembrance
of me afterwardes; now you being one of
mine, & this coming from me, I nothing
doubt of yor louing acceptance of it, for
my sake; though in it selfe, vnworthy to
haue a roome in y^r Librarye, or to come into ye veiw of any Iudicious eye, y^t may
soone spye more faultes, y^n leaues; yet I
know you would in y^r owne goodnes,
pdon & excuse, all defectes therein, y^t
comes from me, a weake vnlearned woman; who being so neare vnt you, you
will gently censure, & beare it all. But
indeed it is so falsly printed, as w^thout
it ba corrected, you will meet wth many
absurdities, wch by some may be imputed
vnto me, though not by you; therefore
I haue a little helped ye most faulty
places, desiring you to do ye like by this,
(in ye other 2. bookes. Now I hope of
one Comfort, wch you will vouchsafe me,
at my earnest request, y^t you will not
faile, to make daily vse thereof to Gods
seruis & glory; wch I beleeue will turne
to y^r owne happines, in drawing
downe all blessings from God vpon
you, as is desired by,

yor most affectionate
Gvanmother, Eliz Cramond

VIRTVTE HONOS

ACQVIRITVR

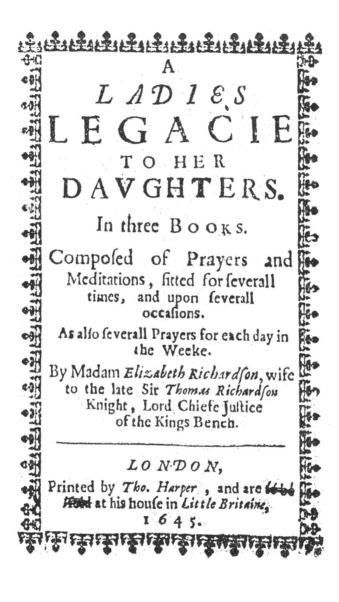

A
LADIES
LEGACIE
TO HER
DAVGHTERS.

In three BOOKS.

Composed of Prayers and
Meditations, fitted for severall
times, and upon severall
occasions.

As also severall Prayers for each day in
the Weeke.

By Madam *Elizabeth Richardson*, wife
to the late Sir *Thomas Richardson*
Knight, Lord Chiefe Justice
of the Kings Bench.

LONDON,

Printed by *Tho. Harper*, and are to be
sold at his house in *Little Britaine,*
1 6 4 5.

The Contents of the Prayers contained in these three Books.

Book I.

A 3   Book

The Contents.

Book II.

The Contents.

Book III.

The Tytle is A Mothers

LADIES LEGACIE

TO HER *Sixe*

DAVGHTERS.

Her latter to them.

Y dearly beloved Daughters (of which number, I account my two fons wives, my daughters in law, the Counteffe of Marlborough, and Mrs. Francis Afhbournham, to be mine alfo) affuring my felfe of your loves and kinde acceptance, I prefent this little Booke unto you all, which being mine, I hope you will carefully receive it, as comming from my love and affection towards you, and that you will pleafe for my fake, the more to imploy it to your good; to which I will (while I live) daily adde my prayers and bleffing for your prefent and future happineffe: and that this my poore labour may prove a happy furtherance to all your good endeavours towards vertue and piety: Therefore let me as a Mo-

A   ther;

ther intreat and prevaile with you to esteem so well of
it, as often to peruse, ponder, practice, and make use
of this Booke according to my intention, though of it
selfe unworthy; for you shall finde your greatest happinesse will be in the true feare, constant love, and faithfull service of Almighty God, which never faileth of
comfort and reward. he being the only and most liberall
giver of all good gifts and blessings, both spirituall and
temporall; to whose infinite mercy and gracious guidance, i most humbly commend you all, and daily will
doe the like in my prayers so long as I live. And further, most deare hearts, consider, That these Petitions
are presented to a most bountifull and Al-sufficient
Lord, that vouchsafeth in Christ to make us his adopted children, and to be our Gracious Father, who gave
his only Son for us, in whom he will deny us nothing:
And greater benefits then here are asked, cannot bee
received; therefore give me leave, since I have such
great interest in you, to perswade and obtaine of you
all, often to beg these blessings of God, by these prayers
faithfully offered up unto his Majesty: Whereby you
shall glorifie his holy Name, make your selves eternally blessed, and bring much joy and comfort to

Your most affectionate

Mother,

ELIZ. ASHBOURNHAM.

1

I *Had no purpose at all when I writ these books, for the use of my selfe; and my children, to make them publicke; but have beene lately over perswaded by some that much desired to have them, Therefore I have adventured to beare all censures, and desire their patience and pardon, whose exquisite judgements may finde many blameworthy faults, justly to condemne my boldnesse; which I thus excuse, the matter is but devotions or prayers, which surely concernes and belongs to women, as well as to the best learned men: And therefore I hope herein, I neither wrong nor give offence to any, which I should be very loath to doe.*

✗ y͡f *I would suffer* y͡n *to be Printed.* ✗

This Booke was written at Chelsey *in the yeare* 1625. *by* E. A. *at the Duke of* Buckinghams *house, a part whereof was lent me by the good Dutches, my most honoured Lady, when the great sicknesse was in* London.

A 2

A Letter to my foure Daughters, *Elizabeth, Frances, Anne*, and *Katherine Ashbournham*, of whom three were then unmarried, only *Anne* was married to Sir *Edward Deering* Knight and Baronet.

My deare Children:

I Have long and much grieved for your misfortunes, and want of preferments in the world : but now I have learned in what estate soever I am, therewith to be content, and to account these vile and transitorie things to be but vaine and losse, so I may win Christ the fountaine of all blisse, wishing you with me, to condemne that Which neglecteth you, and set your hearts and affections on better subjects, such as are above, more certain and permanent ; and feare not but what is needfull for this present life shall bee supplyed by him who best knows our wants : and had it not been for your sakes (whose advancements love and nature bindeth me to seeke) I had prevented the spite of my enemies, and forsaken the World before it despised me : But though I am so unhappy as to be left destitute, not able to raise you portions of wealth, yet shall I joy as much to adde unto the portion of Grace, which I trust, and pray, that God will give to each of you, to whose mercy I daily commit you, nothing
× *so refrained my faith from* × doubting,

doubting but that he will receive you into the number
of those fatherleſſe he graciouſly taketh care of, if you
omit not to ſerve and depend upon him faithfully, for
he never faileth them that truſt in him. God is as free
and ready to give as we to aſke, and contrary to the
World, he grows not weary of importunate ſuters, but
often deferreth his bleſſings to make us the more earneſt
for them. Neither hath the Lord withdrawn his favour
ſo from us as to leave us utterly deſolate to deſpair, but
hath graciouſly raiſed us comfort by honourable friends
to be carefull and deare parents, unto us, whom God
preſerve, and ſhew mercy to them and theirs, as they
have done to us. And here I ſend you a motherly remembrance, and commend this my labour into your loving acceptance; that in remembring your poor mother,
you may be alſo put in minde to parforme your humble
duty and ſervice to our heavenly Father, who hath
created us to his owne glory and ſervice; and all we can
performe, comes far ſhort of what we owe unto him; yet
is he well pleaſed, if we returne (for all his mercies) but
obedience, and the ſacrifice of praiſe and calling upon
his holy Name. Now prayer being the winged meſſenger to carry our requeſts and wants into the ears of the
Lord (as David ſaith) he will praiſe the Lord ſeven
times a day, and prevent the light to give thanks unto
God; and indeed, who can awake to enjoy the light
and pleaſure of the day, and not begin the ſame with in-
treaty of the Lords gracious direction in all things, and
deſire of his bleſſing upon us, and all that we have or
doe? Or how can we poſſeſſe or hourely receive ſo many

favours and benefits from God, and not offer unto him
an evening sacrifice of thanksgiving ? Or who dares
adventure to passe the dreadfull night, the time of ter-
ror, and yeeld themselves to sleep, the image of death,
before they are at peace with God, by begging pardon
for their sins, and craving his protection and care over
them in the night ? I know you may have many better
instructers then my self, yet can you have no true mother but me, who not only with great paine brought you
into the world, but do now still travell in care for the
new birth of your soules, to bring you to eternall life,
which is my chiefest desire, and the height of my hopes :
And howsoever this my endeavour may be contemptible to many, (because a womans) which makes me
not to joyne my sons with you, lest being men, they misconstrue my well-meaning ; yet I presume that you my
daughters will not refuse your Mothers teaching (which
I wish may be your ornament, and a crown of glory to
you) who I hope will take in the best part my carefull in-
dustrie, for your present and future happinesse, towards
which I have not failed to give you the best breeding
in my power, to bring you to vertue and piety, which
I esteem the greatest treasure ; and sure I am, it leads
you to him that is the giver of all good things, both
spirituall and temporall ; to Whose infinite mercy I
most humbly commend you, who I trust will fulfill
all your necessities, through the riches of his grace,
and make you perfect in all good workes to doe his will.
And the God of peace sanctifie you throughout,
that your whole spirits, soules and bodies, may bee

kept

kept blamelesse unto the comming of our Lord Jesus Christ, which shall bee the end-lesse joy of your most loving Mother,

1 Thess. 5. 23.

Eliz. Ashbournham.

A Preface, or inducement to Prayer.

THe great God, and Lord of Heaven and Earth, whose wee are, and whom only we ought to serve, hath not left himselfe without witnesse : For as much as that which may be knowne of God, is made manifest unto us, for the invisible things of him, that is his eternall power and Godhead, are seen by the creation of the world, being consi-dered in his workes, to the intent wee should bee without excuse.   Also the infinite love of God is shed abroad in our hearts, and set out towards us in the most gracious worke of our redemption, in that Christ died for us being sinners, and when we were enemies, God re-conciled us unto himself by the death of his only begotten Son, whom God sent into the world that wee might live

A 4   through

Acts 17.
24.27.8.
Cap. 23.
14.17.
Rom 1.
19,20.

His power
Godhead.
Rom. 5.5.
8 9.

His love,
Redemp-
tion.
Jo. 3. 16.
Jo. 4. 9. to
3. 16.
Jo. 15, 23.
10. 15.

Chrifts
love.

through him, and be faved by his life,
greater love then this can none have,
to lay downe his owne life for us. Now
there are three fpeciall things amongft
many that doe alwaies binde and urge
us to the acknowledgement of God, to

His bene-
fits.
Of our
fins.

the love of his Majefty, and the often
calling upon his holy Name, *viz.* Firft,
the multitude and greatneffe of his benefits towards us, for which we ought
to give him continuall thanks. Second-

Our mife-
ries and
neceffities

ly, the infiniteneffe of our grievous fins,
for which we muft of neceffity daily
aske mercy, and pardon from him.
Thirdly, our owne manifold miferies
and infirmities, for which we are con-
ftrained to feek reliefe and remedy. The
firft of thofe *David* confidered, faying,

Pfal. 116
12,13.

9.1.

What fhall I render unto the Lord for all
his benefits towards me? I will take the
cup of falvation and call upon the name
of the Lord, I will praife him with my
whole heart all the daies of my life. All
his Pfalmes are full of thankfgiving. To
the fecond, Chrift inviteth us faying,

Matth.11.
28.

1 Jo.2.1.
2.1.

9.

Come unto me all ye that are weary and
heavy laden, and I will eafe you. If any
man fin, we have an advocate with the
Father, *Jefus Chrift the juft* : He is the
reconciliation for the fins of the whole
world:

world : And if wee acknowledge our
sinnes, he is faithfull and just to forgive,
and cleanse us from all unrighteousnesse.
For the third, wee are incouraged by
God himselfe, saying, Call upon me in
the day of trouble , so will I deliver
thee , and thou shalt glorifie me ; for
he will have mercy upon us, and heal all
our infirmities ; and when wee are in
misery,he saveth and delivereth us.Now
for the performance of our duty in
thankgiving, the blotting out of all our
offences ,and the release of our miseries,
with the continuance of Gods grace
and favour in all things , the chiefe and
only way to find and obtain all,is rightly
to seek , and truly to serve the Lord by
prayer,who is the author and fountain of
all goodnes,grace and mercy. Every good
gift comming from above,even from him
that freely saith, Aske, and yee shall receive; seek, and yee shall finde; knock,
and it shall be opened unto you ; for hee
that is Lord over all, is rich unto all that
call upon him in truth; and the prayer of
the faithfull,avails much, if it be fervent;
for faithfull and devout prayer is a continuall intercourse and communion betwixt the Lord and us ; and it is like *Jacobs* ladder, by which our prayers make

Psal. 50.
15.

Isy.

Matth. 8.
17.

our

our wants afcend unto God, and his mercie defcend downe upon us; for with the heart man believeth unto righteoufneffe, and with the mouth we confeffe unto falvation; but take heed in fending up thy defires, prefer the good of the foule, before the pleafures or content of thy body; and fet thy affections on things that are above: Firft, feeke the Kingdome of God and his righteoufneffe, and all other wants fhall be fupplied by his mercie, according to his will, and our neceffities. And when thou entereft into the houfe of God, take heed thou offer not unto him the facrifice of fooles, but before thou prayeft, prepare thy felf, thy heart and tongue, as *David* did, left thou tempt God to difpleafure : Be not rafh with thy mouth, nor let thy heart be hafty to utter a thing before God : But ere thou prefume to prefent thy felf, or fervice unto the Lord, meditate upon thefe three things: Firft, of the reverence we owe to the great Majefty of God, in whofe prefence we are, and to whom we muft fpeake; this brings humility and lowlineffe of fpirit, which makes us acceptable unto him. Secondly, of our knowledge and beliefe of the Lords fweet and gracious promifes, which caufeth

Col. 3. 2.

Mat. 6. 33.

Col 3. 1.
Ecclf. 4.
17. 18. 11.

Pfal. 108.
1.

Pfal. 104.

Efay 65.
24.
Job 15. 16.

cauſeth boldneſſe to come unto him, with ſure confidence of being heard. Thirdly, of our unworthineſſe, and what apprehenſion we have of our owne wants and miſeries, and the great neceſſity of Gods helpe and mercy to relieve us. This makes us to know and hate our ſelves, and to love and honour God, in whom is all our help, hope, and happineſſe; therefore with devout reverence, zeal, humility, and true faith, flye unto his mercy, and ceaſe not to call often (as *David* did) ſeven times a day upon the holy Name of the Lord, Pſal. 119. 164. by whom we ſhall bee ſaved, Rom. 10. 13.

---

§ 1. *A preparation to Prayer.*

O Everlaſting feuntaine of all goodneſſe, and well-ſpring of grace, without whoſe ſpeciall aſſiſtance, we are altogether unapt and unable to performe any duty or ſervice that may be acceptable unto thee: Vouchſafe therefore (deare Lord) to helpe mine infirmities, who cannot of my ſelfe pray as I ought, but let thy holy Spirit direct and teach me truly to call upon thy divine Name, with a penitent and faithfull heart, an humble, contrite, and lowly ſpirit, a quiet, obſervant and recollected minde, freed from the vanities and cares of this vilde world, or the love of

this

this prefent life; fo as I may dedicate my felfe wholly unto thee a living facrifice, faithfully and devoutly to ferve thee now, and all the daies of my life. O Lord, make mee to lift up innocent hands, with a pure heart; and guide thou my lips with wifdome, and fet a watch of grace before my mouth, that my tongue may not offend thee at any time, but duly praife thy glorious Name, now and for ever, Amen.

2. *A Prayer to the Holy Ghoft.*
for grace.

O Gracious Lord Holy Ghoft, I humbly befeech thee to fit and prepare my heart, and to direct and affift me in the right and true performance of this duty and fervice now of prayer towards my God: Thou underftandeft my difability of my felfe to any goodneffe: neither know I how to pray as I ought, except thy holy Spirit teach me: Therefore I earneftly and humbly pray thee to give mee thy grace and true fpirit of prayer, that fo I may now and at all times offer up my petitions and praifes, in calling upon thy great and glorious Name, in a right faithfull and acceptable manner, to the glory of God, and the good and comfort of me thy poor fervant, in foul and body, with the furtherance of my falvation, through Jefus Chrift, my bleffed and only Saviour, Amen.

3. *A*

3. *A Preface to any Prayer.*

O My Lord , in all humility I come unto thee, the giver of all grace; thou knoweft my un-aptneffe to any goodneffe, thou haft given me an earneft defire to pleafe thee , make perfect thine owne good worke , and grant me a ready will and ability to performe my humble duty herein a-right,that fo I may fincerely and intirely love,fear and honour thee above all , and moft carefully o-bey thy bleffed will in all things : Good Father, let thy manifold mercies cover my infinite offen-ces from thy All-feeing eyes , and by thy grace caft all vaine thoughts, and finfull hindrances out of my foule, that thy facred Spirit may direct my fpirit to pray with due reverence to thy Majefty, confidence in thy mercy, with fure truft in thy promifes, and feare of thy judgements. And that I may offer up all my fupplications unto thee,with unfeigned zeale, true faith, humility and repen-tance : Sweet Lord, make me heartily thankfull unto thee for all thy bleffings, and let all my peti-tions tend to thy glory ; fo as I may finde favour with thee, that thou wilt be gracioufly pleafed to heare and accept of me and my prayers, that they may enter into thy prefence, and obtaine pardon of all my fins paft, with grace to ftaine my life in true obedience to all thy Commandements, the reft of my daies to come ; that fo my laft end may

be

be happy, and after death I may enjoy the felicity to live with thee, my Lord, for evermore, through the merits and passion of my only Saviour Jesus Christ. So be it.

---

4. *A confession of sins, with a prayer for remission, taken partly out of the prayer of* Manasses.

Almighty Lord God of our fathers, who hast made heaven and earth, with all the ornaments thereof, who hast bound the sea by the word of thy commandement, whose terrible and glorious Name all men doe feare, and tremble before thy powerfull judgements; for the displeasure of thy great Majesty cannot be borne, and thy angry threatnings against sinners is importable, and who can stand in thy presence when thou art offended? But yet (O Lord) thy mercifull promises to penitent sinners are unmeasureable, and unspeakable; for thou art the most gracious Lord, full of mercy and great compassion, and of long suffering, that desires not the death of a sinner, but that he should repent and live, who of thy great goodnesse hast promised to give repentance and forgivenesse to them that sinne against thee, that they may be saved. Now thou therefore (most dear Lord) who camest not to call the righteous, but sinners to repentance (of
whom

whom I am the chiefe)thou of thy infinite mercy
(I trust) hast appointed repentance and remission unto me, whose sins are in number above the
sands of the sea, or the haires of my head; I have
committed much evill, and have omitted to doe
the good I ought, for I have neglected all my duty and service towards thee, and am not worthy
to be called thy servant, nor to behold the height
of heaven, or to looke up unto the place where
thine honour dwelleth, for the multitude of mine
iniquities have bowed me downe, and as a weighty burden are too heavy for me; I am depressed
with the load of my sinnes, and oppressed with
the feare of due punishment for them; for I have
justly provoked thy wrath (O God) and multiplied my transgressions before thee : I have not
done thy will, neither thy holy Commandements
have I obeyed. Now therefore (O my Redeemer) to thee I humbly bow the knee of my heart,
imploring thy mercy, and beseeching thee of
grace : I will confesse my sins against my selfe,
and will not hide my unrighteousnesse from thee:
I have sinned (O Lord) I have grievously sinned, &
I acknowledge my manifold offences; for which
I have nothing to answer, but (like the Publican)
Lord be mercifull unto me a miserable sinner :
Wherefore I most humbly intreat thee to forgive
me, my sweet Saviour forgive me, and destroy
me not with mine iniquities : be not angry with
me for ever, neither condemne me in thy displeasure

sure to the lower part of the earth, and reserve not evill for me hereafter : But (deare Father) make me of that blessed number, to whom thou imputest not their faults, and whose sinnes by my Saviours righteousnesse are covered; for thou art the God of the just, and the God of them that will repent, and in poore me, thou wilt shew all thy goodnesse and pity; for thou wilt pardon and save me that am so vilde and unworthy, even of thine owne great grace and mercy : Therefore I will turn my steps into thy waies, and will seeke thy will, and obey thee with my whole heart : I will praise thee all the daies of my life, and for ever : And let the heavens and the earth praise thy eternall Majesty; for thine is all glory for ever, Amen.

---

5. *A Prayer for the Lords day, before*
we goe to Church.

O Eternall God, most high Creator; preser-ver and disposer of all things : to thee is due all praise, honour, and worship, for thou art our gracious Lord, the only author of all our good, by whom we live; move, and have our being.   O with what humble reverence, and devotion ought we to prepare our ears and hearts, to hear, receive and performe any thing which concerneth thy

most

most sacred Majesty; and even to take heed unto
our feet when we enter into the house of God,
that our waies may not offend thee : Neither
ought we to presume to take thy holy Name into
our mouths , except we endeavoured our selves
to be reformed by thy lawes. Thou, O God, art
Lord God of Sabbath , and hast inobled this day
by the glorious resurrection of thy Son our Lord
Jesus , and by the guidance of the Holy Ghost in
thy blessed Apostles, and Catholicke Church, hast
ordained it for thy publicke service , honour and
worship : so make me to serve thee therein with
due feare and reverence. I most humbly beseech
thee to sanctifie my heart and soule to the true
performance of thy blessed will in rightly observing the same; and leave me not unto my owne
weaknesse and disability , who can of my selfe
neither thinke well , nor doe any thing that is
good, for all my strength and righteousnesse is in
Christ my Redeemer : Assist me therefore (sweet
Saviour) with thy Spirit of grace to cease from
sin , and all worldly workes , or earthly cogitations this day, that may withdraw me from thy fear
and service : And give me an attentive eare to
hearken diligently to thy divine word: Open my
heart as thou didst the heart of *Lydia*, that with
true understanding, I may receive, and faithfully
keep the same , with a conscionable care to practise what I shall learne thereby, devoutly calling
upon thy most holy Name , and using due reve-

B   rence

rence in all my actions before thee : And good
Lord, blesse thy servant whom thou hast appointed this day to instruct and direct us in thy word
and will; open to him the doore of utterance,
and give him the true understanding of thy holy
word, that according to thy gracious pleasure all
may be saved that come unto the knowledge of
thy truth, and that he may be faithfull in thy service, rightly to dispose thy divine mysteries, and
to teach in faith and verity : And grant that I
may heare with due attention, and resolve to follow and practice all good instructions, with true
intention to thy glory, and the furtherance of my
salvation, through Jesus Christ our Lord, Amen.

6   *An entrance to Prayer.*

O God of mercy, thou wilt not the death of a
sinner, but rather that he should turne from
his wicked waies and live : Vouchsafe to knit
(deare Lord) my soule unto thee, that I may truly
feare thee, and unfeignedly love thee, dedicating
my selfe unto thy service, and setting mine affections and desires in all true obedience, to seeke
above all things thy glory, thy Kingdome, and
thy righteousnesse; that so all thy graces may daily
increase in me, and my humble and unperfect service in calling on thy holy name, may grow daily

C   more

more faithfull and fervent, now and at all times to be acceptable unto thee, through the merits of thy deare Son, and my only Saviour, in whom thou art well-pleafed, Amen.

---

7. *A short thanksgiving at the first sight of the morning light.*

O Lord, I bleffe thee for my health, reft and prefervation this laft night, and all my time paft: And now moft humbly pray thee give mee grace fo to fpend this day, that fome glory may redound unto thee by my fervice, fome benefit and good unto them with whom I live, by my example, and fome further affurance unto my felfe of thy favour, and my eternall falvation, through Jefus Chrift my Redeemer, Amen.

---

8. *A private morning Prayer.*

Eternall God, and my moft loving Father, in all humility of foule, and unfeigned acknowledgement of my bounden duty, I humbly prefent my finfull felfe here before thy Throne of grace and glory; befeeching thee to ftrike an awfull reverence into my heart, left my prefumption and want of due respect towards thy great Majesty; should turne my prayers into sinne.   And seeing without faith it is impossible to please God, indue me, good Lord, with true faith to believe, and apply unto my owne soule, all thy most gracious promises in Jesus Christ, whom thou hast appointed to be my righteousnesse, redemption, and the reconciliation of my sins; his pretious bloud I know is allsufficient to satisfie thy just displeasure against me, and to make me, through him, to appeare pure, holy, and acceptable before thee: But of my selfe, alas, I confesse that I am poor, wretched, miserable, and wholly corrupt both in soule and body, the chiefe of all sinners, guilty of the breach of all thy Commandements, such an one as in whom is no goodnesse, and to whom there is nothing due, but shame and utter confusion for ever, O Lord give me a lively apprehension and sight of my wofull estate, that with true faith, contrition, and unfeigned repentance, I *may* lay hold on thy mercy and gracious pardon, in thy beloved Son my only Saviour, humbly beseeching thee (O dear Lord) to accept his blessed death, as an absolute discharge for all mine offences; so as my sins may never be imputed unto me, but that all my infirmities may be healed by his wounds; for I know thy mercy is above all thy works, and thou delightest not in the death of a poor sinner. Therfore I will wait for thy salvation, relie on thy gracious promises, and trust in thee for ever and ever, Amen.   9. A

9. *A thanksgiving.*

I Will praise the Name of the Lord becaufe he is good, and his mercy endureth for ever; for thou haft many waies extended thy great goodneffe towards me, thine unworthy fervant, which I acknowledge with all humble thankfulneffe; for who am I, that thou fhouldeft be mindfull of me in mercy, to refresh me this night paft with quiet reft, and to defend both my foule and body from all the perills thereof; preferving me by thy gracious providence all my life hitherto, from many evills and juft punifhments that my finnes have deferved, fhould have fallen upon me: And thy mercies are renewed every morning: O Lord, thy compaffions faile not, but thou haft multiplied thy benefits towards me, both fpirituall and temporall; which I befeech thee for Chrift Jefus fake ftill to continue and increafe, efpecially thy favour in beftowing all fpirituall graces on mee needfull to falvation: O let thy holy Spirit direct me in every word and good worke, and fill me with the fruit of righteoufneffe, fo as I may have a holy care this day and ever, to live as in thy fight, and to ftudy to pleafe and obey thee in all things, with reverence and feare, in a pure, holy, and blameleffe converfation. O God, knit my foule unto thee, and create a new and upright heart within me, and fanctifie me throughout, in foule,

B 3 body,

body and spirit , that I may give up my selfe a living sacrifice, holy and acceptable unto thee, and
may be preserved from all sin and evill , this day
and for ever : crucifie my sinfull flesh with the
lusts thereof, and withdraw mine affections from
the love of this vile world , and fix my desires on
things that are above , where my Saviour sitteth
at thy right hand, who is my treasure , my hope
and help, with whom I trust to live for evermore,
Amen.   And further I beg all these blessings in
the name , merits and mediation of Jesus Christ,
concluding in that perfect prayer which he hath
sanctified and left us saying, Our Father, &c.

---

10. *A Prayer for the afternoone.*

MOst Gracious God, and my mercifull Father.
in Jesus Christ : how exceedingly are wee
wretched   creatures bound unto thy excellent
Majesty for that unspeakable priviledge which
thou vouchsafest unto mortall man , to have free
liberty and accesse (through Christ) unto thy
gracious presence, there to unfold our woes , to
powre out our soules, and lay open our griefes and
desires before the immortall God , who is ready
to heare, and art both able and willing to relieve
and helpe us ? This imboldneth me (unworthy
wretch) to present my person and petitions unto
thy

thy grace, and to call upon thy holy name through thy beloved Son : Lord let the words of my mouth, and the meditations of my heart, be alwaies right and acceptable in thy fight, my strength and my Redeemer; for thou knowest my nature and substance; being but flesh and bloud, how corrupt and fraile it is, so that I am not of my selfe able to performe any holy duty as I ought, neither to will or do any thing that is good, without thou grant me the assistance of thy holy Spirit, to sanctifie my thoughts, to guide my tongue, and to helpe my infirmities : what am I but dust and ashes, a most vile and miserable sinner, conceived and borne in iniquity, and my transgressions are daily multiplied, adding sinne unto sinne till they be innumerable? how have I mispent this present day, the sinnes whereof, may justly provoke thy heavy displeasure against me, having throughout my whole life, committed all evill, and omitted all good, and have neglected the performance of my bounden duty and service towards thee upon every flight occasion; and which is worst of all, custome of sinning, hath seared up my conscience, and deprived me of the true fight and sense of my sins and wofull estate, and bred such a fearfull hardnesse in my heart, that I cannot duly repent as I ought, and as the greatnesse of my fault requires? Thou hast called often, and sought to reclaime me, and hast waited to have mercy on me, but I have refused,

and

and hated to be reformed, careleſsely neglecting
thy infinite patience, long ſufferance, and goodneſſe towards me.   But now to thee, O God of
mercy, I bring my heavy laden ſoule, caſting my
ſelfe downe at thy feet, beſeeching thee, O Lord,
to receive me to grace and favour, and reject me
not as I have deſerved, but convert thou me, and
I ſhall be changed : make me turne unto thee in
true contrition, that thou maieſt returne unto me
in gracious compaſſion, to forgive all mine iniquities, remit my ungratefulneſſe, and remember
my offences no more.   O waſh and cleanſe my
ſinfull ſoule in the pure bloud of that innocent
Lambe, that I may feele the vertue of his death, to
ſlay all ſin in me, and the power of his reſurrecti-
on to raiſe me to newneſſe of life, in true obedience to all thy Commandements ; and with a
child-like love, feare to offend thee, ſtriving to
pleaſe thee in all things, that ſo I may obtaine favour and mercy in thy ſight, both for thy bleſſing
in this life, and eternall ſalvation after death,
through thy dear Son, and my only Saviour Jeſus
Chriſt, Amen.

---

11. *A ſhort Prayer for night.*

O God, the fountaine of all goodneſſe, I humbly and thankfully acknowledge, although I
am altogether unworthy of the leaſt of thy manifold

fold mercies; yet have I great experience of thy
infinite goodnesse, bounty and favour, both towards my foule and body all my time paft, **this**
day, and alwaies, preserving me from all the **evills**
which fin and nature have made me fubject unto,
with a gracious fupply daily ever fince I was born,
of all things needfull for this prefent life : For all
which I humbly bow the knee of my heart and
foule unto thy glorious Majefty ; but efpecially
for all thy graces furthering my falvation by Jefus
Chrift , I bleffe and praife thy moft holy name,
yeelding all poffible and hearty thanks for all thy
benefits vouchfafed to mee , the continuance
whereof I humbly beg at thy gracious hands,
commending and committing my foule and body
into thy mercifull protection this night and ever,
praying thee to preferve me therein from all perills, fin or evill, for thou Lord only keepeft mee
in fafety : now ftretch out thy wings of grace
and mercy over me, that while fleep feizeth upon
my body, let not fecurity oppreffe my foule, but fo
fanctifie all outward refrefhings unto me, as thereby I may bee the more fit and able to ferve thee
faithfully all my life to come , that taking quiet
reft, becaufe thou Lord fuftaineft me, I may alfo
when this life ceafeth, lay downe my head in thy
peace, and be made partaker of thy glory, through
thy mercies and Chrifts merits, with the affiftance
of the bleffed Spirit. To whom, O Father, Son,
and Holy Ghoft, be all praife, power, dominion,
and

and glory now and for ever, Amen : Continuing
my prayers further as Chrift hath taught us , faying, Our Father, &c.

12. *A fhort Prayer in bed before fleep.*

DEare Lord, receive me this night and alwaies,
into thy gracious protection , to give mee
now health , fafety , and reft , if it be thy will :
And dear God , when I fhall enter into my long
fleep of death, vouchfafe to fanctifie, and prepare
my foule for eternall life , by the affiftance of thy
grace and holy Spirit , before thou call me away
hence ; and grant me a happy and bleffed departure out of this world , that thou maieft receive
me into thy favour and mercy, to be with mee in
my death, that I may dye in the Lord, and reft in
peace, and obtaine a bleffed refurrection, that fo
I may be accepted to live with thee, to praife thy
great and holy name for ever, Amen.

13. *A Prayer before the receiving the Sacrament
of the Lords Supper.*

O Moft fweet Saviour Jefus Chrift , and my
deare Lord, who art the authour and finifh-
er of my faith, redemption, and falvation, the life
and

and food of my soule : I most miserable sinner,
presuming nothing at all on mine owne merits or
worthinesse, but trusting wholly in thy infinite
mercy and goodnesse, doe feare and tremble to
appeare before thy Majesty, or to come unto the
table of this heavenly banquet : But thou Lord
Jesus who graciously callest me, and all heavy
laden sinners, accept in mercy the will for the
deed, in that I am unworthy and ill prepared to
presume into thy presence; and vouchsafe me the
assistance of thy divine Spirit; I humbly beseech
thee, in this holy action, that my duty and service
therein may bee acceptable in thy sight : And
powre down thy heavenly blessing upon this thy
holy Ordinance of thy Word and Sacraments,
that they may be effectuall to revive, strengthen,
and supply in me all sanctifying and saving graces
needfull to the due and right performance of this
sacred duty in an acceptable manner, whereby to
enlighten my understanding with thy grace to the
right knowledge of thee and thy truth; and work
in me a lively true faith, wherewith I may lay
hold and apply unto my sicke soule all the sweet
and comfortable promises and benefits purchased
by the bitter death of my sweet Saviour : Indue
me also with most unfeigned and hearty sorrow
and repentance for all my great and grievous sins
and offences committed against thee; for all
which I most humbly beg thy gracious pardon ;
and grant me such perfect love and charity, that I
may

may sincerely, with all due reverence and devotion, love thee, my God, with all my heart, soul and strength, and may love my neighbour as my selfe, yea my very enemies for Chrits sake, that so I may rightly receive this blessed Sacrament, being prepared by thy grace as I ought to bee : And let, O Lord, thy pretious bloud shed for me, cleanse and wash away all my sins, and the breaking of thy pretious body, heale all the wounds of my corrupt soule, that by the gracious operation of the Holy Ghost, I may be inwardly and inseparably joyned to thee my head Christ; that thou maiest supply all my weaknesse and defects in soule or body, out of thy infinite fulnesse of grace and mercy; that being cloathed with thy righteousnesse, I may be accepted by thee, and through thee; and so be accounted worthy to be partaker of all thy merits, that with the outward signe of bread snd wine, I may blessedly receive the true signified Christ, with all his benefits, and may have grace to hunger and thirst after the spirituall food of Chrits body and bloud, to nourish my soule unto eternall life, and to make me become a new creature in holinesse of living, with all true and humble thankfulnesse, to thy glory and my everlasting salvation : beseeching thee to accept my poor endeavours for perfect performance, and reach forth thy helping hand from heaven to save me, thy unworthy servant, pardoning my sins, and covering my imperfections, with the pure innocencie

nocencie of that immaculate Lambe,
Jelus my Saviour. And ſo I humbly
commend my ſelfe unto thy mercy, who
art able to doe abundantly, above all
that I can aske or thinke; to thee be all
honour, power, and praiſe for evermore,
Amen.

A ſhort meditation, direction, or prepara-
tion before you preſume to enter into the
preſence and ſight of God, to approach un-
to the heavenly banquet, humbly deſiring
this, or the like by prayer. As thou
draweſt near unto the holy table, pray
earneſtly in thy heart unto Chriſt:

THat he will draw near by grace unto thy ſoul, to ſtrengthen thee with
knowledge, true faith, unfeigned repentance, and perfect charity, that thou
maieſt rightly, reverently, and faithfully
receive this holy Sacrament to Gods
glory, and thine owne comfort, and
ſalvation. Now when thou commeſt
to communicate and receive this bleſſed
Sacrament of the Lords Supper: Firſt,
baniſh all vaine and earthly thoughts,
and recollect thy heart to the ſerious meditations,

Know-
ledge of
God and
our ſelves.

Pſ. 14. 23.
1 Jo. 1. 8.
Col. 3. 2.
Rom. 12.
1. 2. & 1.
15.

1 Tim. 2. 4
Humility.
1 Pet. 5. 6.
1 Jo. 2. 2.
& 4. 14. ditations, of that which is the life of the
Sacrament, even the death of thy Savi-
our; and humbly and devoutly present
thy selfe and service to the Redeemer
of thy soule, and Lord of the feast, the
only saviour of mankinde, Jesus Christ
our righteous Lord.   Then apply thy
minde to these contemplations : First,
remember with great reverence the

True re-
pentance.
1 Jo. 9.
Prov. 28.
13. infinite Majesty of God, his mercy,
goodnesse, and justice, in whose presence we are. Secondly, consider thine
owne vilenesse, misery, and unworthi-
nesse, being wholly corrupt both in soul

True faith
1 Pet. 1.
18. 19 21.
2. 14. 1. 3.
21. and body. Thirdly, confesse all thy sins
plainly, for in hiding our sins this work
will not prosper; but with most hearty
and unfeigned sorrow, in all humility
cast thy self at Jesus feet, earnestly begging for pardon, with hatred to all sin,

1 Pet. 2. 22
Heb. 12.
24.
1 Jo. 2. 1. and purpose of amendment : For who
so confesseth and forsaketh their sins
shall finde mercy. Fourthly, trie and
acknowledge thy faith, and stedfast beliefe in Christ Jesus (the blessed Son of

1 Tim. 21 God the Creator) to be the only Saviour
and Redeemer of the world, who dyed

1 Tim. 1. 17. for thy sins, and rose againe for thy justification, and is ascended up to heaven
for thy salvation; where sitting at Gods
right

right hand , he maketh intercession for thee, and powreth downe all graces and blessings upon thee, who giveth himself with all his merits, unto thee in this Sacrament, covering all thy offences with his perfect obedience : So making thee righteous, and leaving thee a pledge and seale of thy future and eternall happinesse, this his holy institution, which the divine word hath sanctified to that end and purpose. Now call to minde the exceeding love of God and Christ towards thee, the one in sending his only deare Sonne, to become man and suffer death : The fifth, in giving his most precious body and bloud , to bee crucified and shed upon the crosse , to satisfie the just wrath of God due for thy sins ; of which this bread broken, & wine powred out (that we see) is a remembrance which we ought often to celebrate, and set our hearts and soules duly and truly, to love and honour this gracious God and Lord, who hath loved us first, and done such great things as to give himself for us. 6. Ponder well in thine heart all the divine mysteries of this holy Sacrament : to which heavenly banquet, Jesus thy Saviour now inviteth thee, taking away thine hatefull iniquities, and

cloathing

1 Tim. 2.
5.

Jam. 1. 17

Sanctifi-
cation.
1 Jo. 17.
19.
Heb. 13,
11.

Gods love
to us.

Our love
to God.

1 Ja. 4. 9.
10.

Jam. 2. 8.

Jo. 15. 12. cloathing thee with his innocencie; so
Charity to to make thee acceptable in the sight of
our neigh- God the Father, and by the gracious o-
bours.
1 Jo. 4. 21. peration of the Holy Ghost, joyning
thee unto himselfe, as thy head, and all
of us in true love one to another, as
members of one body, to walke in new-
Amend- nesse of life the rest of our dayes. 7. And
ment. lastly, forget not to be ever truly thank-
1 Jo. 33. full for these inestimable benefits of God
10,
1 Pet. 4. 2. the Father, of the blessed Trinity; and of
Jesus Christ our Lord towards us, who
hath laid downe his own life to redeem
us, such vile and miserable sinners, all
Thank- which the Holy Ghost applieth unto us.
fulnesse. Infinite mercies, we are never able suffi-
1 Jo. 5. 7. ciently to acknowledge and admire.
Eph. 5. 20. Prepare not thy belly, but thy soule; be-
1 Thess. 5. lieve, and thou hast eaten; this saith St.
18.
Augustine.

x thesa x

---

14. *A thanksgiving after the holy
communion of the Lords Supper.*

OH! blessed and praised for ever, be
the Name of the Lord my God,
who hath done great and many things
for me; and holy is thy gracious and glorious

rious name, and let thy mercy and thy truth (O Lord) never forsake me, but vouchsafe to continue thy goodnesse and loving kindnesse towards me for ever, and say unto my soule thou art my God, my helpe and my salvation for evermore. And now especially (O Lord) as I am infinitely bound, I render unto thy divine Majesty all humble and possible praise and thanks for this present and particular favour shewed unto me thy unworthy servant, in feeding my soule to eternall lfe, with the most pretious food of thine owne sacred body and bloud, blotting out all my sinnes, and sanctifying mee by thy holy Spirit, imputing to me thy righteousnesse, and admitting mee (so unworthy) to be a happy partaker of this blessed Sacrament: The benefit whereof is unspeakable, and the mercy therein unexpressable; only I admire thy goodnesse towards mankind, and magnifie thy great mercy, beseeching thee (my God) as thou hast vouchsafed to accept mee at this holy Table; so (good Lord) let mee not depart without a blessing, but be pleased to receive me into thy gracious care and favour, that I may live and die therein; and give mee grace to spend the rest of my time in a carefull reformation of all evills past, a diligent performance of thy most holy will in all things, and true obedience to all thy Commandements, with a faithfull and right application of all thy mercies and merits; so that I may feele thy bitter passion (O Lord) sweet unto my soule, and

C   by

by the affiftance of thy Spirit, bring forth the fruits
of amendment of life, and moft hearty thankfulneffe all my daies ; that at the end of this life,
I may obtaine a bleffed roome in the Kingdome
of glory, there to praife thy holy name for evermore, Amen.

---

15. *A fhort Prayer for conclufion to any
prayer.*

O God the Father, bleffe and governe my foule
and body, in all things to thy fervice : O
Lord the Sonne my Saviour Jefus, protect me, and
direct me at all times to doe thy will : O holy
Ghoft, bleffed Spirit, preferve mee from falling
into any finne or evill : but inftruct, fanctifie and
lead me into the waies of truth and righteoufneffe,
that I may live in thy feare, and dye in thy favour, and may continue in thy right Church and
true faith unto my end : So that in the home of
my death, and in the dreadfull day of judgement,
I may finde grace in thy fight that thou maieft
pardon and paffe by my fins, and receive me to
mercy through Jefus Chrift, that I may live with
thee my God for evermore, Amen.

16. *A Prayer for the Lords day in the afternoone when you are from Church; being seven humble petitions from a poor sinner to our Saviour Jesus Christ, the Lord and fountain of mercy, prescribed and allowed by sacred Scripture.*

MOst great and gracious Lord, and my only Saviour Jesus Christ, whom the Angels doe admire, all the Saints doe magnifie, and at thy name (O Jesus) doth every knee bow in heaven and earth : I most humbly beseech thee, to have mercy on me that presume to speake unto thee, who am but dust and ashes; yet Lord I beg of thee to forgive all my grievous and manifold offences, and cast all my sins out of thy sight, and not only to pardon all my past misdeeds, but also by thy mighty power and spirit, to slay all sin in me for the time to come. And of thy gracious favour vouchsafe while I live in this world to make mee a blessed partaker in the first resurrection to arise here, from remaining or lying dead in sin, and so the second death shall

1. Remission of sins, and amendment of life.

Luke 18. 13.

Rom. 6. 6.

2. To rise from sin, Rev. 20. in this life

C 2   have

3. In death
Rev. 14. 13
21. 3. 4.
Luke 22.
32. 36.

have no power to hurt me, but by thy grace and affiftance, I may become a new creature in all holineffe of life before thee, that I may daily bee raifed from fin by thy holy Spirit to a new life of grace in Chrift. But when the appointed time of my death doth approach, fweet Jefus leave me not, but keep and deliver mee from that great houre of temptation, when Sathan will fift mee, and feeke my deftruction, · then deare Lord, pray for me that my faith may never faile, neither let my foules enemies prevaile over mee, but make thy poore fervant one of thofe bleffed that fhall die in thee, O Lord, whofe tears God will wipe from their eyes, and they fhall reft from their labours, and their workes follow them. Now, good Iefus, grant

4 The fi ft
judgemēt.
Mat. 25.
34. 41.

alfo in the laft day and houre of death, when I fhall come to my firft account before the Throne of God, and the dreadfull Majefty of the Father; O my Saviour, appeare with mee, that by thy gracious mediation I may finde favour in his fight, and through thee obtaine to bee received into the fociety of thy Saints and fervants ; and alfo by thy infinite mercy and bitter paffion, that I may in and through thee have my fins

covered

covered and pardoned, and may be accounted worthy to escape thy just and
great wrath, which my iniquities have
deserved, and say alwaies unto my soule
thou art my God , and my salvation for
ever. And so I miserable sinner, through
thy merits, sufferings, and unspeakable
mercy, may be made able to stand before
thee the blessed Son of God and man, at
my appearance in thy glorious and awfull presence when thou commest to
judge the world , and hast full power to *in mercy*
save or to condemne us, then looke gracious on me, as one of thine. And sweet
Saviour, I further beseech thee by thine
owne former and free election and meer
grace towards me , vouchsafe in the
dreadfull time of thy great visitation,
that my poore name may be found written in heaven in the booke of life , so as
sin nor Sathan may not bee able to blot
mee out; but that thou, gracious Iesus,
wilt be pleased to acknowledge me (thy
most unworthy servant) to be thine, before God and all his holy Angells. Now
lastly , Lord by thy great goodnesse and
mercy , that I may be received into thy
grace and favour, and so accepted as to
injoy that most happy place and heavenly inheritance of everlasting glory,
grant **C 3** which

5. At the
last judge-
ment,
6. Is after
death.
Rev. 9. 20.
15.

The 7th.
For eter-
nall life,
John 17.
22. 24.
Psal. 16. 11.
Conclusi-
on.

which thou our Iesus hast dearly purchased for us:
that where he my blessed Saviour is, I may live
with him, who loved me so much as to die for me,
and through him being admitted into the glorious presence of God, which is the fulnesse of joy,
at whose right hand are pleasures for evermore:
I shall there eternally serve, praise and magnifie
his most holy name, who liveth for ever and
ever, Amen.

---

17. *A Prayer to the Trinity for direction and acceptance from God, of all our prayers.*

MOst glorious God, and our heavenly Father
in Christ, I most humbly pray thee for his
sake to heare and accept mee, and my supplications that I offer up unto thy Majesty in the name of
thy beloved Son: And I beseech thee sweet Iesus,
in thy love and mercie, which made thee become
our Redeemer, vouchsafe also to be my gracious
advocate, and to direct and receive my petitions,
and present them to the Father; for by and
through thee only, I must obtaine acceptance.
Now further I beg of thee, Lord Holy Ghost,
who best can teach us to pray as we ought, to
take compassion on my frailties and infirmities, to
heale and helpe them, and be pleased to sanctifie
and assist my heart and soule to performe this duty
and

and service at all times , rightly , faithfully , and constantly; to Gods glory, and mine owne comfort and furtherance of my eternall salvation in Chrift my Saviour, Amen.

---

18. *Another Prayer for the afternoon for many*
severall bleffings.

OH moft dear Lord , who knoweft my manifold infirmities , and innumerable miferies : In mercy let thy gracious care and holy hand bee over me now and ever, to guide me into thy right paths,that I may walke in the wayes of thy Commandements , and keepe them with my whole heart unto my end. And vouchfafe, good God, to clenfe and change the thoughts of my corrupt heart from vaine and idle imaginations, to good and godly meditations , which may produce in me by thy affiftance , holy actions agreeable to thy moft bleffed will ; and by thy fpirit let my affections be reformed , and my love withdrawne from the vanities of this vile world, and may bee fixed on heavenly things above, that there may be my heart and only joy, where my Lord Chrift fits in glory at the right hand of his Father ; and fo I may with bleffed *Mary* chufe the better part , to forfake all the world, and my felfe alfo, to follow and heare I efus ; and firft and chiefly fo to feek as
C 4   to

to obtaine that which is most needfull, even thy
glory, O God, thy Kingdome, and the righteousnesse thereof, and leave all other things to be bestowed on me as shall seem best unto thee.   And
Lord grant that my understanding may be inligh-
ned to discerne, imbrace, and practice the holy
workes of thy blessed Spirit, and that my memory
may be strengthned to retaine and make right use
of all the good instruction that I heare or read according to thy will, and make my heart the store-
house of all thy divine precepts, that by thy grace
I may bring forth good fruit in my life ; and make
mee able rightly and reverently, to read and
heare thy holy word, and heavenly will daily as
I ought to doe, and by thy grace to frame my life
thereafter; and direct thou me thy poor servant in
all I goe about to doe that which is best, and most
to thy glory, that howsoever all the powers and
faculties of my soule, or the members or senses of
my body may be decayed or lost by age, griefe, or
sicknesse, for the occasions of this life, yet so Lord
all that is needfull for thy constant service, I beseech thee, continue to my last breath.   And
also be pleased to grant, that my death be neither
sudden, nor unexpected, nor my pains violent,
whereby to be made unable earnestly and faithfully to pray and call upon thy holy name ; but if it
be thy will, give mee knowledge of my death
when thy time is come to call mee out of this
world, and assist me fervently to crie unto thee
                                                    for

for grace and mercie, in the needfull time of
dread and danger; then (deare Lord) fit and prepare me for thy selfe, and give me a blessed departure hence to dye in thee, my Lord, and so I shall
remaine safe and ever happy; and sweet Iesus,
make me pray unto thee with my last breath, and
yeeld up my spirit to God that gave it with praises in my mouth unto my gracious God, the Father, Son, and Holy Ghost. Now vouchsafe,
good Lord, while I live, to indue me thy most unworthy servant with thy grace and holy Spirit,
whereby devout love, and feare of thy Majesty,
with true faith, stedfast hope, perfect charity, and
unfained repentance, with all other saving graces, may be daily renued and increased in mee,
towards thee, to thy glory, and the furtherance of
my salvation through Christ: O sweet Saviour,
who hast performed and suffered great and many
things for mee; deare Jesus, continue thy infinite
favour, and finish thy worke of mercy towards
me the least of thy servants, still to call and draw
me daily unto thee, and make me faithfull, constantly, and wholly thine, in all humble obedience
and true humility to serve thee in uprightnesse of
life, and a holy conversation towards all so long
as I live, and wilt assure my soule, that thou art
my mercifull God, and after death, make me
a happy partaker of thy everlasting Kingdome of
glory. So be it. Amen.

19. A

19. *A Prayer of three petitions, to the blessed Tri-nity, the Father, Son and Holy Ghost, for the spirit of prayer, for repentance and remission of sins, and grace to amend and lead a new life.*

O My Lord Holy Ghost, our sanctifier and comforter, and preserver, the giver of all heavenly gifts and graces, and the directer and assister of us to all goodnesse: I most humbly pray thee to indue me thy poore sinfull servant, with thy true spirit of grace and prayer, to helpe and teach me how to pray as I ought, and to drive a-way, and banish from me in the performance of this my duty, all evill temptations, and wicked hindrances that seek to pervert and withdraw my heart and soule from the true service of my God; and suffer not the world, the divell, nor any his agents to have power over me, or part in mee, to prevaile against me, and to cause God to turn his eare and face of mercy, from hearing and recei-ving my prayers and supplications : but Lord, by thy grace make my petitions now and alwaies right, faithfull, and acceptable to Almighty God, through Iesus Chrilt my blessed Saviour.

But O my God heavenly Father, the originall of all goodnesse, and mercy, who graciously com-mandest us to call upon thee in the time of trouble, that thou delivering us, we may glorifie thee;
what

what greater misery and danger, then a heavy
load of sins that will not easily be cast off, and a
wounded spirit who can beare it? for I confesse
I have most grievously sinned against thee, and
my iniquities are multiplied before thee, as the
starres which cannot be numbred. O Lord, whose
compassion never faileth those that seek and trust
in thee, as thy mercy exceedeth all thy great
workes, so let that through thy deare Son move
thee to releafe mee of this intolerable burthen;
which else will throw mee out of thy presence,
and favour, wherein is the fulnesse of joy; and
presse me down to hell into everlasting torments
amongst the enemies of God and man. Now
mercifull God, who hast pity on thy poore creatures, and delightest not in the death of a sinner.
Lord turne me from all my evill wayes, that I may
be converted unto thee, to feare, love, and obey
thee unto my end : And vouchsafe to pardon all
my transgressions past, and remove my sins from
me as farre as the East is from the West, and bury
them in oblivion, that they may not be able to fe-
parate my God from mee, as far as heaven from
hell : but Gracious Lord, be pleafed to give me, thy
unworthy fervant, the bleffed gift of true forrow
and repentance to falvation, to fit me for thy mercy, and prepare me with grace by the amendment
of all my misdeeds, for thy loving acceptance of
me in thy favour againe, and fay to my loft foule,
I am thy God, and thy falvation for ever ; and fo
                                        thou

thou working in me, both the will and the deed, the praife, honour and glory be only thine, for evermore.

Now fweet Jefus, the fountaine of mercy, and Saviour of all that truft and believe in thee, who gracioufly calleft all heavy laden and penitent finners to come to thee, that thou maieft eafe them; have mercy on me, and heale my finfull foul with thy moft pretious bloud; and thy righteoufneffe I know is alfufficient to cover a world of finnes, if thou pleafe to impute it unto mee. O fhrowd mee under thy innocent wing, that the great wrath I have deferved may never fall upon mee: but vouchfafe, dear Lord, to receive mee finfull creature into thy favour, as thou didft *Mary Magdelin*, to become wholly thine; and be thy faithfull difciple fo long as I live; and ftretch forth thy hand of mercy, as thou didft to *Peter* from finking in the fea; fo Lord fave me thy unworthy fervant, from perifhing in my fins; and by thy affiftance, according to thy bleffed advice, that I may make my peace here, where I have tranfgreffed, before I goe where the utmoft farthing muft bee paid. O Lord, by thy grace make me a new creature, daily to worke out my falvation, with forrow for my time loft, feare to offend again, and trembling at the heavy judgements due unto me, and ftriving to make my calling and election fure, by a holy life and godly converfation both towards God and man all the reft of my dayes. And make mee

caft

caſt utterly off all love of this deceitfull world,
which is but loſt, and my owne vaine deſires that
hang ſo faſt on, and only apply my heart and
ſoule to ſeek after thee and thy Kingdome, with
the righteouſneſſe the reof, and then I ſhall obtain
the end of my faith and hope; even thy glory, and
my owne ſalvation, through thee only dear Jeſus.
my bleſſed Lord and alone Saviour. To whom
with God the Father, and the Holy Ghoſt, three
Perſons, one eternall God and glorious Trinity,
be rendred as is due, all praiſe, honour and glory,
for ever and ever, Amen.

O

---

20. *The concluſion to this booke. A ſhort Prayer
ſo to performe our duties here towards God, that
we may obtaine heaven hereafter.*

OH moſt mercifull Lord God, thou knoweſt
my unaptneſſe to any good : I humbly pray
thee to give me thy poor unworthy ſervant grace
ſo truly to feare thee, as not to offend thee; ſo conſtantly to beleeve in thee, and confidently to relye upon all thy gracious promiſes, in all my troubles and neceſſities; and ſo entirely and ſincerely
to love and honour thee above all things, that nothing in this world may withdraw my minde
from thee, nor any vaine hopes, or earthly deſires
make mee neglect my ſervice to thee; but that I
may

may daily study and strive, rightly and carefully to obey thee my Lord at all times, diligently to seek thee, and know thy will, and faithfully to serve and please thee as I ought to doe as long as I live. For thou, O God the Father, lovedst us first, and sent thy deare Son out of thy bosome to redeeme us, and our sweet Saviour Jesus in his love gave himselfe, and laid downe his owne life to save us from eternall death; greater love cannot bee found then for one to dye for a friend, but thou Lord diedst for thine enemies; much more having now reconciled us to the father, and to thy selfe: I trust being united to thee also by the Holy Ghost, by sanctification and true faith wrought in me by that blessed Spirit, I shall obtaine mercy through the merits and sufferings of my deare Jesus, to live with thee in heaven hereafter, to glorifie the great Name of God, the eternall Father, Son and Holy Ghost, to whom bee all praise and honour for ever; and let heaven and earth, Saints and Angells, and all creatures, give glory to him for evermore, Amen.

Here is one Prayer more which I joyne to those, because it concerned one of my daughters, to whom this Booke belonged, though it was lately penned upon a very strange accident.

G 2   *A*

21. *A thanksgiving to Almighty God, for his most mercifull preservation of my noble kinswoman the Lady Eliz. Feelding, and of my owne daughter, the Lady Eliz. Cornwalleis, from drowning under the Bridge, and was long under water : and one worthy Gentlewoman in the company could not bee recovered. This may serve upon any such fearfull accident.*

MOst Mighty God, Creator of heaven and earth, and the only disposer of all things therein, thou art the defender and protecter of all thy children and servants, and the gracious preserver of all those that depend upon thee : thy power ruleth both by sea and land, and thy all-guiding providence directeth all things in the world, according to thy own high will and good pleasure, and for the good of all them that trust in thee. Whereof thou hast given many, and mee the unworthiest of thy servants; an especiall testimony of thy infinite mercy towards my deare daughter and kinswoman, in that great and miraculous deliverance lately of them, in the dreadfull danger of sudden death by drowning in the Thames; for thou didst mercifully provide and take care to save their lives, whilst they were past sense to take care of themselves, or to call upon thee for helpe : yet beyond all hope, thou didst bring them backe from the gates of death, praised for

for ever be thy most glorious Name; and let neither us, nor any of our generation forget this thy great mercy. Now Lord, make us duly to acknowledge all thy benefits, and let us not passe them out of our mindes without true thankfulnesse for all thy favours continually vouchsafed unto us undeserved: for all which we poor creatures have nothing to returne to thee, but devout love, faithfull service, and carefull obedience, with the humble sacrifice of praise and thanksgiving; which by thy assistance, I will performe towards thee with a gratefull heart, so long as I live, and for ever, Amen.

---

22. *A Petition of the Author for herselfe.*

O Lord; as *Paul* said, he would readily performe the duty in his charge that lay upon him, lest while he preached to save others, himself should become a cast-away: so dearest Lord, I having taken pains to compose many Prayers for the use of others (under my care) to further them in the constant performance of this duty of prayer; which being rightly used, will draw many blessings from thee: Almighty God, I most humbly beseech thee, to heare and receive their supplications, that call upon thee by these Prayers. So, Gracious Lord; suffer not me to neglect my

duty

duty and daily service herein, towards thy Majesty, but make me carefully, rightly and reverently to offer up due praises and prayers, daily unto thee in a faithfull and acceptable manner all the daies of my life. And give me thy poor servant the assistance of thy grace and holy Spirit, to reform all my waies before thee; to suppresse and overcome the corruption of my heart, the vanity of my mind, and to forsake and abandon the love of this vile world, with all the deceitfull vanities thereof, and to cast off those great & superfluous cares and desires after the things of this mutable life, which passe away like a shadow or dream. Wise *Solomon* that had the plenty, and triall of all things under the Sun, tells us what it will prove, only vanity of vanities, and vexation of spirit. Wherefore let me learne with *Paul*, in what estate soever I am, therewith to be content, and to submit with humble patience to thy pleasure in all things thou sendest, who knowest what is best and fittest for me; and keep me for repining and despairing in thy chastisements; for thou canst heale as well as wound, when thou pleasest. Therefore I will dedicate my heart and soule, and all my endeavours unto thy faithfull service, striving to make my calling and election sure, by looking after thee my God, thy Kingdome, and thy righteousnesse, which is the only thing needfull: This grace grant unto mee, O God, for Jesus Chrifts sake, Amen.   *The end of the first Book.*

D   Book 2.

Called,

A weekly exercise of Prayers for each Day.

BOOK II.

The Epistle.

THis Book *I began to write at my house at* Barking *in* Essex, *where I retired my selfe in solitarinesse, after the death of my worthy and dear husband,* Sir Thomas Richardson, *Knight, Lord chiefe Justice of the Kings Bench : who dyed at* Candlemas, 1634.

Where shortly after I finished these Prayers following for my owne private use ; being the fittest imployment for my time, who was then in so much heavinesse.

I call this Book a weekly exercise of Prayer, either for a private person, or in their owne family : To which there are added some other necessary Prayers, very usefull for those particular occasions, whereto they are directed : which I shall be very glad and joyfull, if my children, grand-children, kindred, friends, or any good Christian that shall peruse them, may make a good and right use of them to Gods glory : And I doe most heartily and humbly pray, that God will vouchsafe to heare in heaven, and to receive, accept, and grant their just requests ; to his owne honour, their comfort, and

D 2

my

my great happinesse, who am a wel-wisher, and true lover of their soules in the Lord,

Eliz. Richardson.

To the Reader.

THese *Prayers I composed for the instructions of my children, & grand-children, after the example of my dear parents, Sir* Thomas Beaumont, *and his Lady,* of Stoughton *in the County of* Leicester, *who I thinke were as carefull and industrious to breed up their children (which were living) in the instruction and information of the Lord, to serve and obey God, as any parents could possibly be, which made them take much paines with us, more then is usuall, by their endeavours to bring us to know and feare God, and to keep his Commandements :* Which Solomon *saith, is the whole duty of man. But when parents have done the best, and all we can, it is Gods grace and blessing that must perfect the worke: which I humbly pray him to adde to accomplish my desire, to their eternall happinesse.*

An

A weekly exercise of prayers.

An Exhortation concerning Prayer.

BEfore thou goest to pray : confider ferioufly of thefe three things, which are very neceffary to fit and prepare thee the better for that holy and bleffed exercife : Firft, ponder with thy felfe, into whofe prefence wee come, and to whom we prefume to fpeak, being before the great Majefty of God Almighty.   Secondly , in what manner we pray, and to what end our prayers tend, which muft chiefly refpect the glory of God and his fervice ; and then our owne defires and neceffities, both for foule and body.   Thirdly, weigh well what good. or hurt , what benefit or danger may enfue, by the performing of this duty carefully or negligently.   *Before y^u prayeft prepare thy felfe, & tempt not God.*

---

1 . *A fhort Petition to precede any other Prayers.*

O Lord Holy Ghoft , who knoweft my corrupt heart, and the frailty of my foule, which can performe no good but by thy grace. Vouchfafe, my Lord, to fanctifie, affift and teach me the unworthieft of thy fervants, by thy holy Spirit, to to pray now and alwayes ; that my fupplications may be faithfull and acceptable to my God, to his glory, and the comfort and good of my felfe, both in foul and body for ever, Amen.

2. *A Prayer to God the Holy Ghost, for the true spirit of grace in prayer.*

O God Holy Ghost, the giver of all good gifts and graces, give mee thy true Spirit Lord, who art the comforter and sanctifier of thine Elect : thou knowest my great and manifold infirmities, and frailties ; all which, I humbly pray thee in thy love and mercie to heale and helpe. And Lord give me power, strength, and grace, by thy assistance, to resist and overcome all wicked assaults and temptations of the divell ; that seeke to draw me from God and goodnesse, and lead mee to all evill : but vouchsafe Lord, I beseech thee, still to be present with me in this holy exercise, and indue thy poore servant with thy blessed Spirit and gift of prayer to call upon thy glorious Name faithfully and sincerely, whereby my unworthy petitions (though full of imperfections) may be received and accepted by thee. And Lord, banish all wandring thoughts, and wicked hindrances from my soule, in the performance of this my bounden duty and service, that I owe unto thee, my God, Father, Son, and Holy Ghost : And be pleased Lord, to assist mee now and ever with thy grace to worship thee at all times, in spirit and truth, as thou requirest : and not to present a dead, dull and corrupt offering unto my Lord, of the lips without the heart, or by joyning in my

thoughts

thoughts God and the world, or mammon together, which thou hatest, and so make my prayers
abominable to thy Majesty; for thou hast made
the heart, who ought and must be served and honoured with it. Therefore I humbly pray thee,
to inable me by thy assistance, to offer unto thee,
my God, a holy and living sacrifice, of my selfe,
my prayers, and praises daily, in a right and acceptable manner, not looking so much to the benefit and recompence of reward that shall bee received thereby from thy mercifull hands to my
owne good, but chiefly for the honour and glory
of thy great Name, whose I am, and whom I am
bound to serve, and from whom I have already
received so many great blessings and benefits
both spirituall and temporall: for which I render
most humble and hearty thanks unto thy Majesty.
Now lastly, deare Lord Holy Ghost, I earnestly
beg of thee, daily to unite mee unto thy glorious
head, and only Saviour Jesus Christ, that so I may
performe with true faith, good devotion, humility, and sincerity, this, and all other holy duties
and services, according to thy blessed will and
word, to thy glory and my great comfort; now
and for ever: So be it.

D 4

3. *A short preface before any other Prayers,*
for the Lords day.

Almighty Lord God, in whose glorious pre
sence I am, presuming to take thy sacred
name into my sinfull mouth: before thee, Lord, I
most humbly prostrate my selfe; thou seest the
heart, and knowest our wants before we aske, yet
hast thou commanded us to ask in thy Sons name,
promising for his sake, to grant us all needfull
blessings both for soule and body. O Lord, thou
understandest my great weaknesse and disability,
who can doe no good, but by thy assistance : I
now most humbly pray thee, to keep all evill in-
terruptions from my heart and soule, and so to indue mee with thy true Spirit of grace and prayer,
in performing this duty and service to thy glorious Majesty; that so all my supplications may
now and at all times be right, faithfull, acceptable, and pleasing unto thee; and by thy great
mercy also, prevailing for my good, and furtherance of my salvation, through my only Lord and
Saviour Jesus Christ. Amen.

4. *A Prayer for the Lords day at first awaking.*

O Most glorious Lord God, the high and gracious Creator of heaven and earth, with all
things

things therein; Thou didst finish that mighty work in six dayes, and rested the seventh, commanding thy Church and people of the Jewes to keep holy the seventh day, to thy due service and praise. But our Lord Jesus having finished the redemption of mankinde by his crosse and passion, and bitter sufferings, didst bury that Sabbath in his grave upon that day, and by thy Spirit didst guide thy Apostles and Christian Church to sanctifie and keep holy this first day of the weeke, in perpetuall memory of his glorious resurrection and eternall rest from that labour, and suffering for our redemption, to thy due service and praise; blessed be thy holy name therefore. And now, dear Lord, for all my former neglects of my duty herein; for Jesus his sake, pardon my sinfull breaches of this, and all other thy holy Commandements heretofore: and vouchsafe, O God, alwaies to knit my straying heart, to the true feare of thy great name, to keep me from offending thee, and fill my soul with the infinite love of thy divine Majesty, that I may daily strive to lead the rest of my life in all obedience to thy holy will. And Lord, vouchsafe to inspire me thy most unworthy servant, I humbly pray thee, with thy blessed Spirit, that I may withdraw my minde this blessed day, from all worldly cogitations, thinking my owne thoughts, speaking my owne words, doing my daily works, or going my owne waies; but assist me with thy grace, that I may apply my heart and soule wholly to meditate

tate of thy wonderfull works, and manifold mercies, with thankfulnesse, and to attend thy service either publique or private, with care and faithfulnesse, and to obey all thy Commandements henceforth with diligence, and constantly serving thee all my life to come, that so I may praise and glorifie thee, and thou maiest pardon my sins, and save my poore soule, through thy great and unmerited mercie in Jesus Christ, my Lord and only Redeemer, Amen.

5. *A Prayer for the Lords day in the morning before going to Church.*

My soule praise thou the Lord, and all that is within me praise his holy name, who is most worthy of all honour and glory.

Almighty God, our heavenly Father in Jesus Christ thy beloved Son, who of thy infinite goodnesse by thy great power and divine word, didst in six dayes create heaven and earth, the sea and the whole world, with all things therein, and resting the seventh day, didst blesse and hallow it, commanding all thy people in purity after thine owne image, to keep the same holy to thy due honour and praise; having also given us six dayes for our owne occasions: and after this great and unexpressible

unexpressible worke, thou didst also in thy appointed time accomplish by thy beloved Son Jesus, that happy redemption of mankinde, who were lost by sin, and fallen from thee; which unspeakable mercie and benefit was as upon this first day of the week consummated by the miraculous blessed resurrection of our Saviour, which wee Christians now keep in commemoration of these thy infinite benefits; that according to thine appointment thy servants may rest this holy Lords day, from all worldly affaires to thy honour and glory: blessed and praised now and for ever, bee thy glorious Name, for these thy marvellous workes. Therefore I most humbly beseech thee, O Lord, of thy great mercie, by thy Spirit of grace, to sanctifie mee thy most unworthy servant, both in soule and body; that I may at all times, but especially this Lords day, and upon all other daies consecrated by thy Church to the memory of any of thy blessings, benefits and deliverances, wholly devote my selfe, to thy true feare, holy devotion, and faithfull service, in performance of thy blessed will and commandement: And so thy worthy name may be glorified, my salvation furthered, and thy favour and blessing rest alwaies upon me and mine. And likewise I most humbly pray thee, O God, for thy Son Jesus sake, to forgive all my sins done in my whole life past, in breaking this and all other thy divine Laws, that through the death and bitter passion of my deare

and

and innocent Saviour , which hee suffered to redeem us, thou wilt vouchsafe to be reconciled unto me, thy guilty and sinfull creature; that as this
is a day of rest to thy due praise , so by thy mercy
it may bee a happy day of joy and peace to my
poore soule and conscience , through my only
Lord and blessed Saviour Jesus Christ, Amen,
Amen.

---

8. *A Prayer to be said at the Church, as soone
as we are come into our seat.*

O Lord our God, who art here present amongst
us , thou seest and understandest all things,
and knowest my heart; prepare, sanctifie, and af-
fist my heart and soule, with thy grace, so to be-
have my selfe , both outwardly and inwardly, as
in the presence of thy glorious Majesty, in this
thy blessed house of prayer and hearing thy word,
with such due reverence, feare , humility ; true
faith and devotion, as may be best pleasing and acceptable unto thee , and most profitable and a-
vailable for the good of mine owne soule.   O
God , indue thy servant the Preacher , with thy
holy Spirit , to teach thy saving truth rightly and
sincerely, that it may be powerfull to our edifica-
tion, and effectuall to the beating downe, and ba-
nishing of all sins from our soules , and the en-
creafe

creafe of faith and grace in us that heare him ; to
thy glory , and the furthering of our falvations,
through Jefus Chrift our Lord, Amen.

---

7. *Another fhorter Prayer to the fame purpofe.*

GOod Lord, that knoweft my infirmities, prevent and remove all fin and evill hindrances
and impediments of drousineffe , and wandring
thoughts from me fraile finfull creature, and open
my ears and heart like *Lidiees* to attend and marke
diligently what is taught out of thy moft facred
word. Inlighten, Lord, my underftanding, to
conceive rightly what I heare, and keep my mind
wholly intentive upon thy faithfull fervice, in
hearing thy holy word with true devotion before
thee ; and make my memory retentive of all the
good inftructions that I learne, and give me grace
carefully and confcionably to practice them
throughout my whole life , to the honour of thy
great name , the performance of thy moft holy
will, the amendment of all my faults; and finally,
the falvation of mee thy poore fervant, through
my Saviour Jefus Chrifts merits and mercies,
Amen.

R 2   A

8. *A Prayer after the Sermon is ended, before we go out of the Church.*

MOſt Gracious Lord God, I humbly beſeech thee, to pardon all my ſinfull neglects, defects, and want of due preparation, or any infirmities that have overtaken mee in the performance of my duty towards thee, in this thy houſe, and bleſſed exerciſe of Prayer, and hearing of thy divine Word. And let me not depart out of this holy place without thy bleſſing, whereby my knowledge, faith, holineſſe, and comfort in thee may be daily increaſed in me : And Lord, adde thy grace to what I have now heard, that by thy gracious aſſiſtance, it may bring forth plentifull fruit in me, to the reformation of my life and converſation, in avoiding all evill, and doing all good, which may be ſerviceable and acceptable to thy Majeſty, and beſt pleaſing in thy ſight, through Jeſus Chriſt, my only Saviour. Amen.

A Prayer for the Lords day at night, of three Petitions.

FIrſt, thankfulneſſe for benefits already received, with prayer for the continuance of all Gods mercies. Secondly, for repentance, true faith, remiſſion of ſins, and amendment of life. Laſtly, ſo to live and dye unto God here, that after death, we may live with him in heaven for ever.

8. The

9. The Prayer.

MY foule praife thou the Lord, and forget not all his benefits, which forgiveth all thine iniquities, and healeth all thine infirmities, which redeemeth thy life from death, and crowneth thee in mercy and compaſſion, who provided a ranſome for thee, before thou hadſt being to underſtand thine owne wretched eſtate. Oh, my Lord God! how good and gracious haſt thou ever been in all thy mercies both ſpirituall and temporall towards me, the leaſt and unworthieſt of thy ſervants, before I was borne, and ever ſince, from time to time? Now Lord, I humbly pray thee, in the ſame love and favour, from which I have hitherto received ſo many and great benefits, vouchſafe thou alwaies to continue thy bleſſings unto me, eſpecially in daily renewing all ſpirituall graces in my ſoule, for the true performance of all holy duties and ſervice, in a right and acceptable manner towards thy Majeſty: and Lord, make my humble thankfulneſſe unto thee, appeare in my true obedience of thee in all things, that I may duly praife and glorifie thy name for ever. Now deare God, let not thy mercy in prolonging my daies, encreaſe the number of my ſinnes, and ſo to heap up wrath unto my ſelfe againſt the day of wrath, by drawing upon me due puniſhments for my offences; but merciful God, adde thou grace unto

unto my daies ; and for Jefus fake, forgive all my
finnes paft that I have done before thee in my
whole life time , efpecially in my many breaches
of this holy and bleffed Lords day, which we keep
in remembrance of our Saviours refurrection; with
all my neglects and defects in the performance
of my duties towards thee this prefent day , and
heretofore , according to thy Commandements.
And grant, O God, through thy mercies, and my
3. Saviours merits, that my iniquities may never bee
imputed unto mee ; but Lord , let thy goodneffe,
patience, and long fufferings, lead me to daily and
unfaigned repentance : and give me true faith in
all thy gracious promifes, and by the affiftance of
thy holy Spirit, to bring forth amendment of all my
former faults, with true obedience unto thy bleffed will, and holineffe of living all my life to come:
That fo I may obtaine grace and favour in thy
fight, to prevent and keep mee hereafter from all
fin and evil, or offending thee, my God, in thought,
word and deed ; and direct thou my waies right
before thee , in all godlineffe and uprightneffe of
heart, that I may be enabled through my Lord Jefus Chrift, to doe every good worke , and by thy
grace to live here according to all thy Commandements; and when thou pleafeft to call for mee
out of this wicked world unto thy felfe , Lord affift me with thy fpirit and grace to make a bleffed
end, and to die in thee, my Lord , and fo I fhall
finde mercie through the merits of my Saviour
Jefus,

Jesus, after death to be accepted and received into the Kingdome of heaven , and through Chrift
my Saviour , may bee admitted into thy glorious
prefence,O God,where is the fulneffe of joy,and
at thy right hand there are pleafures for evermore,
of which Lord make me a happy partaker , when
this life is ended. Amen, Amen.

---

10. *A Prayer for Munday to God the Father,*
at firft awaking.

o Lord

I Will praife thee,with my whole heart,for thou
haft dealt lovingly with mee. Bleffed and praifed now and ever, be thy moft glorious Name, O
my God, heavenly Father , for all thy great and
manifold mercies and bleffings,both fpirituall and
temporall in foule and body, vouchfafed unto mee
thy moft unworthy and finfull fervant , before I
was borne, and hitherto, this laft night , and all
my life paft; for thy favours have ever been right,
good and gracious towards mee , having done
great and many things for mee , prayfed be thy
moft holy Name , who haft been my only ftay,
fuccour, helpe and comfort in this world;and thy
infinite mercy in Ghrift, is all my hope and confidence,for the life to come. Now Gracious Lord,
who haft been my good God and guide from my
youth , have pity upon my infirmities : and for

E   Jefus

Jesus sake, forgive all my sinnes that I have committed before thee in my whole life past, and let thy mercy and truth, never leave me nor forsake me, neither in life, in death, nor in the last judgement, but be pleased by thy Spirit , to say alwaies unto my soule, especially at my death, thou art my God and my salvation, for in thee will I trust so long as I live, and for ever.   So be it.

A short supplication before the weekly Prayers.

11. *A morning Prayer for Munday to God the Father.*

HEare me when I call upon thee, O God of my righteousnesse, have mercy upon mee, and hearken unto my prayer.   Most Gracious Lord God, and my heavenly Father, in Christ Jesus my Saviour; thou knowest my great and grievous infirmities, that I can of my selfe neither will nor performe any good, nor think a good thought, but by thy grace ; therefore I most humbly pray thee to indue mee thy poore unworthy servant with thy holy Spirit, whereby these and all other my prayers and petitions , that I presume to offer unto thy Majesty , may by thy assistance be made in a right manner,   and in an acceptable time, when thou wilt please to be found of me, and graciously to heare and receive me and my supplications

tions. And now vouchsafe, dear God, to sanctifie, prepare and assist my heart and soule, with thy true Spirit of grace and prayer, to drive away all vaine and wandring thoughts, sluggish dulnesse, and all evill temptations out of my minde; and knit my heart and soule to the true feare of thy great Name, and to the devout love of thy divine Majesty; and teach mee with all due reverence, and such true humility and devotion, as is fit to appear in thy sacred presence, that I may rightly, faithfully, and humbly, now and at all times, call upon thy holy Name as I ought to doe, and daily pray unto thee, O my blessed Lord God, who hast awaked mee in health and safety to this daies light, which I most thankfully acknowledge, with all other thy blessings and benefits, both spirituall and temporall, bestowed on me thy sinfull servant, from time to time; beseeching thee of thy infinite mercy alwaies to continue them unto me. And as thy gracious providence hath brought me to begin this new day, so Lord, by thy power defend me therein from falling into any sin or evill, to offend thee; but give me grace at this present to performe, and ever continue to lead a new, a holy, and an upright life in thy sight, all the rest of my daies to come, to frame my heart, and reforme my waies (in all true obedience hereafter to thy most holy will and Commandements. And further, I humbly praise thy glorious Name, for thy gracious preservation of me and mine, and all o-

ther

ther thy benefits vouchſafed me the laſt night, and all my life paſt unto this inſtant houre, having hitherto given me healtb, maintenance and ſaiety; which, I pray thee, whilſt I live, ſtill to vouchſafe me, and make me truly thankfull to thee for all thy mercies; and let thy benefits never ſlip out of my minde, but that I may daily and duly acknowledge them to the true praiſe of thy moſt holy Name. And grant me grace to ſpend the reſt of my time to come more carefully and faithfully then I have formerly done, to ſeeke, ſerve, feare, love, obey, and pleaſe thee my Lord, in all things as I ought to doe, ſo that it may bee more then meat and drinke unto me, to doe the will of thee my heavenly Father. And I moſt humbly beſeech thee, O God, the fountaine of mercy, to forgive and pardon all my ſinnes and offences paſt that I have committed againſt thee, either in ſoule or body throughout my whole life; Lord blot them out of thy remembrance, with the moſt pretious bloud of thy deare Son, my only Saviour Jeſus Chriſt; and grant through thy mercies, and his merits, and ſufferings, that my iniquities may never be imputed unto me. But vouchſafe, O God, now and ever, to keepe me thy poore ſervant, as the apple of thine own eie from all ſin and ſhame, and hide mee under the ſhadow of thy wings from falling into any evill or danger this day; eſpecially, O Lord, preſerve mee alwaies from the great wickedneſſe of committing any preſumptu-

ous

ous fin before thee, and from the fearfull finne a-
gainft the Holy Ghoft (which is unpardonable)
and from the dangerous fins of negleƈt towards
thee, hardneffe of heart, fenfeleffe fecurity, or falling into wicked defpaire, whereby I may prevent my foule of thy mercy in Chrift for my falvation.   But, good God, direƈt thou my thoughts,
defires, words, and deeds to be ever agreeable to
thy moft holy will, and obedient to all thy Commandements, that I may henceforth live before
thee with an upright heart, daily ftudying and
ftriving to ferve and pleafe thee in all things, fo
long as I live, that after death, I may praife and
magnifie thy Name in heaven among thy Saints
and fervants, for ever and ever.   Thefe great
mercies, O gracious God, with all other thou
knoweft needfull for me, either for this life or the
life to come, I further beg of thee, in the name,
merits and mediation of thy deare Son, and my
fweet Jefus, concluding in that perfeƈt forme of
prayer, which hee hath taught us, faying, Our
Father, &c.

12. *A Prayer to God the Father for Munday night*

O Lord my God, how excellent is thy name in all the
world, who haft done great workes, and brought
mighty things to paffe.

ALmighty Lord, and my heavenly Father in
Chrift, moft high and mighty God, Creator
and   E 3   poffeffor,

possessor, preserver, and disposer of heaven and
earth, and all that is therein, the fountaine of
grace and mercy, and Father of light, from whom
commeth all good and perfect gifts: I most humbly pray thee of thy great goodnesse to give mee
thy poore sinfull servant, thy grace and holy Spirit, to direct my heart and all my waies aright in
thy sight, and to guide me in the paths of truth and
righteousnesse; and Lord, lead mee into that
streight way, and through that narrow gate,
which bringeth unto life eternall; that so of thy
infinite mercie through Christ, I may enter in
(though most unworthy) with them that obtaine
grace to finde it, and there to live with thee, my
God, in joy and blisse for evermore. And further, I yeeld and render unto thee, my Lord, all
humble and possible praise, honour, and thankes,
for all thy great and manifold mercies and benefits, spirituall and temporall, vouchsafed unto me
thy most unworthy servant in soule and body
from time to time; and also for thy gracious preservation of me and mine, and all other thy blessings bestowed upon me this day past, and all my
life hitherto. Now, good God, for Christs sake,
I humbly pray thee, to forgive and pardon all my
sinnes and trespasses that I have committed before
thee, inwardly or outwardly in soul or body, by
thought, desire, word or deed, this present day,
or any time of my life heretofore. Mercifull Father, wash away all my sinnes out of thy sight,

                                                with

with the moſt pretious bloud of that All-ſufficient ſacrifice, the innocent Lamb of God, Jeſus, who was ſlaine for our tranſgreſſions : hide all my ſins in his wounds, and bury them in his grave, ſo as they may never bee able to riſe in judgement a-gainſt me, either to accuſe or to condemne mee. But Lord, make me of that bleſſed number, whoſe ſinnes thou wilt cover, and whoſe iniquities thou wilt pardon. And vouchſafe alſo to forgive my omiſſion of all thoſe good deeds I ought to have done, and my ſinfull negleċt in the true perfor-mance of all duty and ſervice that I owe unto thee; eſpecially my wicked negligence in calling upon thy holy Name, and daily praiſing thee for all thy mercies : and likewiſe I beg pardon for my often omitting, or ſlightly performing this du-ty of praying unto thee as I ought, now and at all times; which Lord give me grace more carefully, faithfully and devoutly to perform towards thee, by the aſſiſtance of thy holy Spirit ever hereafter, that ſo of thine infinite mercy thou maieſt bring mee to that eternall Kingdome, which thou haſt prepared; O God the Father, before the world be-gan, for all that truly love and beleeve in thee, to thy great praiſe and honour, and my ſalvation in Chriſt, through thy mercy, O bleſſed Lord God, to whom be glory now and ever. Amen.

E 4   13. *The*

*13. The conclusion for Munday, to be said last,
or in bed.*

O My God, I most humbly commmend and commit my selfe both body and soule, my children and grand-children, my kindred, friends and family, and all that doth belong unto me, here or else where, with all my fellow members in thy whole Church, into thy most gracious protection and preservation, this night and alwaies. Good God, I beseech thee, vouchsafe to blesse, sanctifie and keep our soules and bodies in thy true faith, feare and favour, with safety, this night, and to our lives end. Amen.

⌃ Catholick

---

*14. A Prayer at first awaking, for Tuesday,
to our Saviour Jesus Christ.*

MY soule shall magnifie thee, O Lord, and my spirit rejoyceth in God my Saviour, who hath done and suffered great and many things for me, blessed be thy most holy Name for thy infinite benefits and blessings, both spirituall and temporall bestowed upon mee thy unworthy sinfull servant from time to time. And chiefly (Gracious Lord) for thy accomplishment of my redemption before I had any being : who didst vouchsafe to

come

come into the world amongst evill men, and to be borne of a Virgin, to take the shape and nature of man upon thee, and in our flesh didst work and performe all righteousnesse to bee imputed unto us; and also submitted thy selfe to suffer the most bitter and ignominious death of the Crosse, to free us from that eternall death, which our sinnes have deserved; and also rose againe from the grave the third day, to overcome sin, death, the grave, hell and Sathan, with all other things for us. And so thou, sweet Jesus, art become our reconciliation, redemption, righteousnesse, and justification, with hope also through thee of salvation and glorification hereafter. Of all which thy inestimable benefits, I humbly pray thee, O Lord my Saviour, of thy infinite mercy both in this world, and after this life is ended, to make me thy poor unworthy servant a happy partaker amongst thy Saints and servants, that I may live hereafter with thee and them, to praise and glorifie thy Name, my deare Jesus, for ever. Amen.

15. *A Prayer for Tuesday morning, to God the Son, our Redeemer.*

I Know that my Redeemer liveth, and shall stand the last day upon the earth, to judge the world in righteousnesse, and all the people with equity.

O

O sweet Iesus Christ, who art my Lord and perfect Saviour, the beloved Son of God, the blessed Redeemer of the world, the only searcher of mans heart, before whom all things are manifest, all desires knowne, and from thee no secrets can be hid: Lord cleanse and reforme the thoughts of my wicked corrupt heart, by the inspiration of thy most holy Spirit, to purge my heart, soul and conscience from all sin, evill, and dead works, rightly and faithfully, to feare and serve thee, the true and living Lord, that I may unfainedly love thee, and constantly praise and magnifie thy holy and blessed Name all the daies of my life, and for ever. Now, Gracious Iesus, grant that the words of my mouth, and the thoughts, and meditations of my heart, in these and all other prayers and petitions that I make unto thy Majesty, may bee alwaies guided by thy blessed Spirit, and that all my waies and actions, be directed according to thy holy word, and so by thy merciful assistance, all things I goe about, shall be ever right and acceptable in thy sight, O Lord God of truth, that art my strength and my Redeemer. And deare Saviour, who knowest the infinite corruption of my wretched nature, and my unaptnesse to all goodnesse, vouchsafe to draw and knit my heart and soule, to thy true feare and faithfull service, and suffer no worldly respects, regard of persons, nor any pleasures, to withdraw my minde, or hinder my soule from the true performance of my daily

duties

duties and service towards thee, my God, with
due observance of thy great Majestie, faithfully,
devoutly and constantly serving thee, and calling
on thy holy name, now and at all times, and daily worshipping thee in spirit and truth, as thy
selfe hast commanded. And be thou pleased, dear
Lord, by thy grace, to guide and direct my heart,
soule, and body, with all my desires, waies, and
workes, according to thy owne good will and
pleasure; for I humbly commend and commit my
selfe, my children and grand-children, with all
belonging to mee, and all things that any way
concerneth me, to thy most gracious protection,
direction, and disposing, now and ever. And I
humbly pray thee, O my sweet Iesus, so to prevent me with thy holy Spirit, that I bee led into
no temptation this day by the divell or his evill
agents, the vaine world, or my owne corrupt
flesh, neither suffer any sinfull thoughts to possesse
my soule; but assist me, I beseech thee, to set a
watch over my heart and waies, and before my
mouth, and set a seale of grace and wisdome over
my soul, and upon my lips, that I offend not with
my tongue, or in my actions, either against thee
my God, my neighbour or my owne soule; but
Lord, make my heart cleane and upright before
thee, and keep me from falling into my former
sins againe, but indue me with grace so to number
my daies, that I may apply my heart to wisdome
and goodnesse, and daily endeavour and strive to
                                                    lead

lead a new and godly life in thy fight; and make me firme, stedfast, and conftant in thy right Church, faving truth, and true faith unto my lives end, to live and die therein; but if I hold any errors contrary to thy will and word (O Lord) speedily convert my foule unto thee, and shew me the paths of life, and teach me thy truth, and suffer me not to slide from it, but so long as I live here, conftantly to set my whole heart, foule, and delight, to feek, to ferve, to love, and to fear thee, my Lord, in all true obedience, humility, repentance, and purity, with stedfast faith in thee, and true holineffe of living, as is required of thy children and fervants, through the affiftance of thy bleffed Spirit, and the bleffing of thy heavenly Father, who liveth and reigneth with thee, three Perfons, and one true eternall God, bleffed for ever. Amen. Concluding my humble petition, with that perfect prayer, which Chrift our advocate hath fanctified, and taught us saying, Our Father, &c.

x yͤ͟ o x

---

16. *A Prayer for Tuefday at night to our bleffed Saviour, for my felfe and children.*

O Sweet Iefus Chrift, that art both God and man, my bleffed Saviour, Redeemer, and Mediator, who underftandeft all things, and feeft what we want before we aske, and knoweft beft

what

what is in miserable mortall man, that is made of
earth, how corrupt my nature and subftance is,
how many and great my frailties and infirmities
are, and how fubject I am to fall into all manner
of evill both in foule and body, if thy grace uphold
me not: therefore I moft humbly befeech thee, O
Lord, to receive me and mine now and ever, into
thy provident and gracious care, to protect and
direct us in all our waies to doe thy blefled will,
and to live in all thy holy feare, to fave and guide
us waking from all finne and fhame; and to keep
and defend us fleeping from all perills and dangers either of foule or body, that fo by thy mercie
we may reft in peace and fafety this night, and alfo awake in thy grace and favour, and doe all
things to thy honour and glory, and may live and
dye thy true and faithfull fervants; and after death
vouchfafe, dear Lord, by thy metits and fufferings
to give us eternall life with thee in heaven,
which thou haft dearly purchafed for us. Now
fweet Jefus, vouchfafe to induc and affift mee
with thy grace and holy Spirit, that I may be able
rightly, faithfully, and confidently (as I ought to
doe) to cry and pray unto thee, my God, for
grace and mercie, that I may finde favour in thy
fight, and that my truft in thee may never ceafe,
that fo I may obtaine true contrition for all my
cffences, and pardon for my fins paft, with all faving graces for my falvation both in life and
death, and affured hope of everlafting life when
this

this is ended, through thy pretious death and bitter
passion, sweet Iesus my Saviour.　Now, good
Lord, indue me with grace, to fit and prepare my
soule as I ought, before my day of death approa-
cheth, that I be not taken unprovided; but assist
me with thy blessed Spirit to worke in my heart a
true and lively faith, to lay fast hold upon all thy
mercies, merits, and gracious promises, and rightly to apply them to my owne soule.　And further
give mee, I humbly pray thee, unfaigned repentance and remission of all my sinnes, with other
needfull graces for the performing of all holy duties to thy Majestie, that so I may be inabled rightly and faithfully to serve and please thee while I
live here; and also make me carefully to fit and
prepare my soule for thy mercifull acceptance,
before thou call me to thy selfe out of this vale of
misery; and give mee grace daily to die unto this
world, and forsake it while I am in it, that I may
live more and more in true holinesse and righteousnesse before thee; and so I shall obtain blessednesse here to be directed by thee in all things,
and to have thy protection over me to die happily
in thee, and live eternally with thee, who art my
only Saviour and Redeemer, Iesus Christ the
righteous, to whom be all glory for ever and e-
ver. So be it.　*x vnto thee x*

17. *The*

17. *The conclusion for Tuesday, to be said at night or in bed, to the Son, for my selfe and children.*

MY sweet Iesus, by thy grace and holy Name, keep mee thy poore servant, and all mine from all sinne and shame, and by thy bitter death and passion, save us from thy great wrath, and endlesse damnation, and by thy powerfull resurrection, raise us daily from sin to grace and newnesse of life, and by thy glorious ascention, draw me thy unworthy servant continually to heaven after thee by a holy life and godly conversation; and of thy great mercie, after death, restore me to be where thou art, and make me partaker of thy everlasting salvation; and in all my troubles, sorrows and distresse, doe thou my griefes redresse, and be my blessed consolation; and vouchsafe to receive me this night and alwaies into thy mercifull preservation : for now I will lay me downe in peace, and also rest and sleep, because thou Lord, dost only mee sustaine, and wilt in safety keep : for on thee alone I wholly doe depend, who art all my hope, helpe, comfort, and confidence, sweet Iesus my Saviour. Amen.

18. A

18. *A Prayer for Wednesday to the glorious Trinity at first awaking.*

GReat is our God, and worthy to be praised, I will speake of all thy marvellous workes, for thou hast done great things, and holy is thy Name.

To thee O God, heavenly Father, our gracious Creator of all things; with God the Son, that blessed Redeemer of mankinde, and God the Holy Ghost the sanctifier of thine elect; unto thee, O Lord, three Persons, one true and everliving God, be given and rendred as is due by mee, and all other thy children and servants, all humble and possible praise and thanks, now and ever. For I thy most unworthy servant, doe humbly and thankfully acknowledge, that I finde thy blessings and benefits both spirituall and temporall, sleeping and waking, daily and howrely, to be renued towards me, for which I blesse and magnifie thy holy Name, especially for those spirituall graces thou hast vouchsafed unto my soule from time to time, before I had any being, for my election by the whole Trinity, and my creation by God the Father, which thou didst fully performe in thine owne innocent person : but chiefly in that infinite love token unto mankinde, of God the Father in ordaining and sending thy deare Son out of thy bosome into the world; and thou, O Christ,

✗ ut my redemption wrought by
thee sweet Jesus my Saviour ✗   in

in comming amongſt wicked men, to put thy ſelfe
into their cruell hands for our redemption, and ſo
become our righteouſneſſe, juſtification, and ſalvation, which thou haſt dearly purchaſed for us
with thy own bloud. And ſince I was borne, O
bleſſed Spirit, for my continuall preſervation, and
daily ſupply of all needfull bleſſings for my ſoule
and body, eſpecially for my vocation, and calling
to the right knowledge of God and his ſaving
truth, with ſome meaſure of true faith, ſanctifica-
tion, and regeneration from ſinne to grace, all
wrought in mee by the holy operation of thee
Lord Holy Ghoſt ; by whom alſo we are united
unto our Lord and head Chriſt Jeſus, from whom
Lord let me never be ſeparated. Now vouchſafe
O God, ſtill to continue all thy mercies towards
me ; and chiefly in giving me daily a ſupply and
increaſe of all heavenly gifts, and ſpirituall graces, whereby I may be able rightly, faithfully,
and conſtantly, to feare and love, to ſeek, ſerve,
and pleaſe thee my God, in all things as I ought
to doe; that ſo I may obtaine thy grace and favour
(by thy aſſiſtance) to live a holy life here according to thy will, that thou of thy infinite mercie,
Almighty God, and glorious Trinity, maieſt make
me partaker of thy heavenly Kingdome of glory
hereafter. Amen.

19. *A Prayer to the Trinity for Wednesday morning.*

O God the Father of heaven, the gracious Creator of all things, the righteous judge, that searcheth the heart, and trieth the children of men, and beholdeth all our waies, and knowest my substance is but dust, flesh and bloud, and my nature as it is corrupted by sin, is of it selfe, earth-ly, sensuall and divelish, and can merit nothing from thee, O Lord, but condemnation.   Deare God, the originall of all goodnesse, I most humbly beseech thee to have mercy upon mee miserable sinner, and enter not into judgement with thy poore servant, for no flesh living is righteous be-fore thee ; neither reward me after my wicked-nesse, for I am a wretched and most sinfull crea-ture, and have done exceeding much evill in thy sight; but I humbly pray thee, O God, for thy dear Son and my Saviours sake, to withdraw thy great wrath and heavy displeasure from mee, which my sinnes have justly deserved; and if it be thy will Lord release my present afflictions, which now and long have lain upon me : and vouchsafe also to prevent and remove those weighty judge-ments, that hang over my head for my iniquities, that by thy unspeakable mercies I may escape them ; yet if thou please further to visit mee with fatherly chastisements for the amendment of my

faults

faults; Lord give me wifdome and patience to beare all things as I ought to doe, without offence towards thee, and by thy grace to make the beft and righteft ufe of all thou fendeft, fo as in the end they may turne to thy glory and the furtherance of my falvation in Chrift my Lord. O God the Son, Redeemer of mankinde, who didft vouchfafe to bee borne of a woman, to become man for our redemption, and cameft into the world to feek and fave all thofe that were loft by fin, that they might live by faith in thee; which Lord grant unto me, fweet Jefus my Saviour, and have mercie upon me a wicked finner, to forgive and pardon all my finnes and offences that I have done before thee all my life paft in thought, word and deed; and impute not my iniquities unto me, neither deftroy mee with my tranfgreffions, nor let thy heavy difpleafure referve evill for me hereafter: but deare Lord, of thy great goodneffe grant me thy poore fervant true faith, and unfeigned repentance, with thy gracious remiffion of all my trefpaffes, and wafh my finnes out of thy fight with thine owne moft pretious and innocent bloud, which thou didft fo freely fhed for our redemption; naile all my offences upon thy croffe, and bury them in thy grave, fo as they may never be able to come in judgement againft mee, either to accufe or fhame me in this world, or to condemne and confound mee in the world to come, for thy mercies fake, fweet Jefus my Savi-

F 2

our;

our : But I moſt humbly beſeech thee , O Lord,
to ſanctifie and cleanſe my heart and ſoule from all
ſinne and evill, by thy holy Spirit , that I may be
upright in thy ſight , to reforme all my waies
before thee, and let thy grace ~~and holy Spirit~~ lead
mee into the paths of truth and righteouſneſſe all
my life, that after death thou maieſt of thy infinite
mercy bring me to that everlaſting inheritance of
happineſſe which thou haſt ſo dearly purchaſed
for us with thine owne bloud , in whom is all my
truſt, who art my only Saviour, Mediator and Advocate. ~~for ever.~~ O God the Holy Ghoſt , our
comforter , preſerve and ſanctifie thou my heart
and ſoule, that I may unfeignedly love thee, truly
feare thy holy Name, and faithfully ſerve , pleaſe
and obey thee , as I ought to doe now and all the
daies of my life : And vouchſafe, O bleſſed Spirit, to inſtruct and inlighten my ſoule and under-
ſtanding, with the true knowledge, devout love,
and ſtedfaſt beliefe of thy ſacred truth, and keepe
me therein for ever.   O Holy Ghoſt , vouchſafe
to make thy ſeat and dwelling in my ſoule , and
let thy holy Spirit take full poſſeſſion of my heart,
and abide alwaies with mee to fill me with all ſaving graces, whereby I may bee preſerved from
falling into any ſinne or evill , and bee inabled to
doe all good that may be beſt pleaſing unto thee,
and to performe all duty and ſervice (by thy aſſiſtance) in an acceptable manner unto my gracious and Almighty God, the Father, the Son, and
                                            the

the Holy Ghost, three Persons, and one ever glorious Trinity, to whom be rendred all praise, honour, power, and thanks, as is right due, for ever and ever. Amen.

---

20. *An evening Prayer to God the Holy Ghost for Wednesday.*

O God the Holy Ghost, blessed Spirit, by whom we are sanctified and sealed unto the day of redemption, and by whose holy operation, we are joyned unto our blessed Lord and head, Christ Jesus; from whom let nothing in heaven or earth ever separate me : And mercifull Lord I humbly pray thee, cast me not in thy displeasure out of thy care and favour for my sinnes, and withdraw not thy grace and holy Spirit from me, neither forsake me, nor leave me to my selfe, who am wholly subject to all wickednesse. But I most humbly beseech thee, to creat in me a new, a clean, an upright, a faithfull and perfect heart in thy sight, to walke in all true holinesse before thee, as thou requirest, all my daies to come; and good Lord, daily renue thy grace, and a right holy spirit within mee, to sanctifie and cleanse my soule from sinne, to preserve mee from falling into evill, and to guide me into the waies of truth and righteousnesse. Now dear Lord, marke me thy

F 3

poore

poore servant for thine owne, and prevent mee
with thy grace that I never grieve, despight, or
neglect thee my God in any thing, neither to resist or quench the good motions of thy holy Spirit
in my heart at any time; but I most humbly pray
and desire to bee led and directed in all things by
thee, who best knowest my frailties and infirmities,
that I can (of my selfe) neither will nor performe
any good at all, much lesse call upon thy holy
Name as I ought, all my best works and endeavours, being full of imperfection and corruption;
but I humbly beseech thee, good Lord, to accept
in mee the will for thee deed, the affection for the
action; and vouchsafe to heale and helpe my great
disability to any goodnesse, and teach, and assist
me rightly, faithfully and constantly, to pray unto thee my God, now and at all times according
to thy holy will, and daily to call upon thy great
Name in truth and sincerity. And be pleased, O
Lord Holy Ghost, to prepare, assist and lift up my
heart and soule towards thee, and bend downe
thine eare of mercy to heare me, and vouchsafe
thou blessed Lord, to make request by thy grace
in mee, with such inward and faithfull devotion,
humility, sighs and groans as cannot be expressed,
that so my supplications may bee acceptable to
God my heavenly Father, through the merits and
sufferings, of my dear Saviour Jesus, and the holy
working of thee O God the Holy Ghost, my comforter,

forter, who art the fanctifier and preferver both
of my foule and body ; I humbly pray thee to in-
flame my heart and fpirit with fervent zeale and
unfeigned devotion to the true and conftant performance of all duties and fervices that I owe unto thee my God. And vouchfafe Lord, by thy
holy Spirit to infufe into my foule everlafting and
devout love towards thy Majefty, with Chriftian
charity towards all my brethren, thy children and
fervants : And Lord, put thou a right and ftedfaft
hope into my heart that my truft in thee may never
faile, till I have attained to the eternall felicity,
which God the Father hath prepared, and our
bleffed Saviour hath purchafed, and thou bleffed
Spirit by thy holy affiftance wilt bring us unto, to
glorifie the Name of my God in heaven hereafter
for ever. Amen.

21. *The conclufion for Wednefday at night, to
the bleffed Trinity.*

MErcifull God, heavenly Father, bleffed Son,
and Holy Ghoft, who haft appointed the
night for all mortall creatures to take reft, without which our weake natures cannot fubfift : I
am now in health by thy gracious providence, by
thy favour, and laid downe in my bed, which re-
prefenteth the grave, and by thy mercie hope al-

so to take quiet rest and sleepe, that is the image of death, from which I know not whether ever I shall awake againe to this worlds light, for my life dependeth on thy good pleasure; therefore I most humbly pray thee of thy infinite mercy, O God, to forgive all my sins past that I have committed against thee, this present day or heretofore, through the merits and sufferings of my Redeemer Jesus; and vouchsafe heavenly Father to bee reconciled unto mee, thy most guilty sinfull servant, in and through thy dear and innocent Son, who is my righteous Saviour: And grant while I live here, that in Christ I may hereafter live to thee, and thy faithfull service; and when I sleepe, Lord let me safely rest by thy blessed preservation, and by the assistance of thy holy Spirit, that I may continue in thy true faith, feare and favour with a good conscience unto my last breath; that so if thou call me away this night, or any other time in my sleep, thou wilt in Christ pardon my sinnes, and after death receive my soule to thy grace and mercy, to remaine with thee for ever, and may praise thee, my God, everlastingly. Amen, Amen.

22. A

22. *A Prayer for Thursday morning as first awaking to God the Father.*

MY God, I heartily praise thee for my present health, rest and preservation this night and formerly, and safe approach by thy providence to this light. I humbly beseech thee, vouchsafe this day and alwaies, to bee my present helpe in all dangers, and my mercifull God to pardon all my sinnes and wickednesse, that I have done heretofore, and to prevent and to protect mee by thy grace and favour from falling into any sin or evill to offend thee hereafter; and direct me by thy holy Spirit in all things I goe about, to doe that which is acceptable in thy sight (through Christ) and to the best for my owne soule. Deare Lord, give me thy sinfull servant thy grace, whereby I may be able rightly and faithfully to seeke, serve, and please thee my God, as I ought to doe, this day and at all times throughout my whole life: These great blessings I beg of thee, O God the Father, by thy gracious assistance, in, and through, and for the sake of thine owne deare Sonne, and my only Saviour, Jesus Christ the righteous. So bee it.

23. *A*

23. *A Prayer for Thursday morning to God the Father.*

MOst mighty God, and my mercifull Father, the giver of all good gifts : grant mee thy grace and the light of thy countenance, to guide mee this day and ever , to walke in thy paths of truth and righteousnesse all my life, and to runne in the way of thy Commandements unto my end; for thy beloved Sonne hath taught us before all things to seek that which is most needfull , even the Kingdome of God , and the rightousnesse thereof, and then our heavenly Father will supply all things else which he knoweth to be necessary for us : Good Lord, make me (with *Mary*) to choose the better part, to seek, heare, and follow our Saviour Jesus, and let that never bee taken from mee thy poore servant. To which end , I humbly pray thee, O God, to weane and with-draw my heart and soule, from the cares, love or liking of this vilde world, and all the vanities thereof, all which like a dream and shadow fade away. : And Lord, drive all wicked thoughts out of my minde , and banish covetous desires (the root of all evill) from my heart, and make me ever consider what it would advantage me, if I could win the whole world, and should lose my owne soule. Therefore I beseech thee, O Lord, by thy holy Spirit, to settle my heart and soul, my desires,

affections

affections, and delight, only upon thee my God,
thy glory, thy Kingdome, thy righteousnesse; and
make me to account all earthly things but drosse
and dirt so that I may win Christ, and attaine to
the excellent knowledge of Jesus my Saviour,
who is the Lord of life, him chiefly, O God, let me
finde and obtaine to be mine, with whom I shall
have all other good things, by thy infinite mercie
I beseech thee, that so I may be able rightly and
faithfully to serve and please thee as I ought, while
I live heare, that after death thou of thy unspeakable goodnesse, maiest make mee partaker of thy
heavenly Kingdome of glory.   And now, deare
God, vouchsafe unto me thy most unworthy servant the grace of daily and unfeigned sorrow
and repentance for all my sins, with a sound sense
and feeling of them in a contrite spirit, with care
to reforme all my former faults in the rest of my
life, and make me strictly to examine my owne
heart, soule, knowledge, and conscience, of all
the evills I have done before thee, and severely to
judge, hate and condemne my selfe for them, that
so I may escape thy great wrath, and may not bee
judged and condemned by thee in thy heavy displeasure, which I am not able to beare; for who
can stand in the sight of thy great Majesty when
thou art angry?   therefore I most humbly pray
thee, good God, in the multitude of thy mercies,
to forgive and grant me thy grace and pardon of
all my sins and offences past that I am guilty of,
for

for thy beloved Sonnes fake, that fo my iniquities
may never be imputed unto me; but Lord give me
true faith to lay faft hold upon thy mercies,and all
thy gracious promifes, and the merits and fufferings of Ghrift, with grace rightly to apply them
to my owne falvation, through Jefus my Saviour;
that fo I may be quit through him,and freed of my
account with thee before I die; and grant that I
may daily die unto the world, and hate all the
vaine preſſures thereof, and may live more and
more unto thee in all righteoufneſſe and true holineſſe of living before thee as becommeth thy
Saints: that fo when thy appointed time is come
for me to enter into my long fleep of death, that
thou wilt be pleafed by thy holy Spirit to fit and
prepare me, and to give me a happy and bleſſed
departure out of this life, to die in the Lord that I
may reft in peace and fafety, and be raifed up by
my Saviour to grace and glory, that thou pardoning all my finnes, and receiving me to mercie,
thou maieft wipe all teares from mine eies, and remove all forrow from my foule,and for Jefus fake
to admit me into thy glorious prefence, ~~and there~~
to enjoy eternall felicitie,and be a happy member
of thy bleſſed Church triumphant to praife thee
there for evermore. Amen.   And the bleſſing
of God Almighty, the eternall Father,the beloved
Son, and the Holy Ghoft, be ever with mee, to
fanctifie, bleſſe and preferve my foule and body
in thy feare and favour, and true faith, ftedfaft

x for thy mercifull acceptance x hope

hope, and perfect charity unto my lifes end. Amen.

---

24. *A Prayer to God the Father for Thursday night.*

HAve mercy upon me, O Lord, and hearken unto my prayer, for I know thou Lord wilt blesse the righteous, and with thy favour wilt compasse him as with a shield. Lord thou lovest not wickednesse, neither shall evill dwell with thee, thou shalt destroy them that speake lies, for thou abhorrest all them that worke iniquity : yet thou desirest not the death of a sinner but that he should returne and live; therefore deare Lord, deliver my soule and save me in thy manifold mercies, for I have grievously sinned before thee, and my iniquities are gone over my head into thy presence, and are too heavy for mee to beare. But I most humbly beseech thee, for thy beloved Son Jesus sake, to give me unfaigned sorrow and repentance for all my sinnes past, which are great and many, and grant me thy gracious pardon and remission for all my offences committed this day or heretofore against thee; and Lord, indue me with true faith to lay hold of all thy mercies, and my Saviours merits and sufferings, with grace to amend, reforme my life, according to thy most holy word and Commandements, all the rest of my

daies

daies to come : to which end Lord give me a foft,
a penitent, upright and contrite heart, with a
tender confcience, and a true and found fenfe and
feeling of all my finnes, infirmities, and fpirituall
wants, with grace earneftly and faithfully to cry
and pray unto thee for mercie and reliefe in all my
neceffities , and chiefly for all fpirituall graces to
my foule.   And as I truft thou wilt awake mee
from the dulneffe of this nights fleep in fafety to
the morning light; fo dear Lord, by thy holy Spirit daily quicken my foule from the deadneffe of
finne, to newneffe of life , and raife me up in mercie hereafter, from the darkneffe of death, unto
light and life eternall , to live with thee my God
for evermore. Now gracious Lord, receive mee
with all that doth belong unto me into thy mercifull protection now and alwaies, to keep and deliver us from all finne and evill , giving us this
night quiet fleep, health and reft if it be thy will;
and grant whether I fleep or wake, live or dye, I
may be wholly thine, and doe all to thy honour
and glory ; that fo both in life and death , Chrift
may be to me an advantage, through thy infinite
mercie, O my bleffed Lord God.   Now I humbly
pray thee, fo to inlighten the darkneffe of my foul
and underftanding with thy grace , that I may fee
clearly the right way to heavenly happineffe, and
by thy affiftance follow hard after it untill I have
attained to it ; and alfo for thy holy Names fake
defend mee from all perills and dangers of this
    ✕ *a daily fupply of* ✕   night

night either to my foule or body, to me or any of
mine, for the love of thy only Son, my deare Saviour Jefus Chrift : for whofe fake, grant me alfo
the guard of thy holy and good Angells now and
ever, that they may pitch their tents about mee
to preferve mee from all my enemies bodily and
ghoftly ; and commit mee Lord to the cuftody of
thy bleffed Spirit to keep me from falling into any
finne or evill, and to guide my waies into the
paths of truth and righteoufnefle, that I may live
in thy holy feare, and dye in thy faith and favour;
and good God, grant that in the howre of my
death, and in the day of judgement, thy dear
Son and my fweet Jefus, may bee my mercifull
judge and Saviour, to pardon and pafle by all my
finnes, and cover them with his righteoufnefle,
that after death I may bee received and accepted
into thy grace and favour, to live and remaine in
joy and blifle eternally with thee my God, Father,
Son, and Holy Ghoft. Now, O God, who canft
doe abundantly, more then I can aske or thinke,
to thee be all praife, honour and glory, for ever
and ever. Amen.

---

25. *The conclufion for Thurfday night*
in bed.

O Lord my God, I thanke thee for all thy mercies vouchfafed unto mee this prefent day
and

and formerly : and now be pleafed, O Lord, by thy holy Spirit to fanctifie me thy poor unworthy fervant, in foule, body and fpirit throughout, to thy right faithfull and conftant fervice all my daies; and affift me with thy grace that I may daily confeffe, lament, hate, leave and amend all my former mifdeeds, and may become faithfully and unfainedly thine in all true obedience and fincere and perfect love toward thy Majefty, both living and dying, and for ever ; that through thy mercy and Chrifts merits, I may be found blamelefle at the appearance of my Lord Jefus, by whom I truft to obtaine to live in heaven with thee, and to bee prefented by my Saviour unto thy gracious acceptance in that great day of the Lord, to remain with thee my God for ever. Amen.

26. *A Prayer for Friday at firft awaking to God the Son.*

DEare Saviour Jefus, have mercy upon mee a miferable finner : Thou immaculate Lambe of God, that kneweft no finne, but diedft for our tranfgreffions, and fhed thine owne moft pretious bloud to cleanfe us from finne : I moft humbly praife and magnifie thy holy Name for all thy mercies who haft done and fuffered great and many things for mee, but efpecially I bleffe thee for
those

those spirituall blessings thou hast bestowed upon me before I was borne, and hitherto. Now sweet Jesus, who knowest my frailty, I doe most humbly pray thee never to leave me to my self, nor to my soules enemies, neither while I live, at my death, nor in the great and dreadfull day of judgement, when all things shall bee made manifest before thee, and it will be wholly in thy power to save or to condemne; then Lord Jesus looke in mercie on me as one of thine, whom thou lovest to the end, to pardon and cover all my sinnes, and receive me into thy grace and favour, for by thee only commeth my salvation, and in thee, O Lord, is my whole trust : Therefore vouchsafe Lord, to continue thy goodnesse, thy favour, and thy loving kindnesse towards me this day and for ever, in forgiving all my iniquities, that I have committed in my whole life past ; and also my sinfull omission of those duties and good workes, which thou hast commanded, and I have wickedly neglected. But I most humbly beseech thee, my Saviour, to indue mee thy most unworthy servant with thy grace and holy Spirit, to direct my heart, and all my waies aright before thee, and preserve me at all times in the sincere and perfect love of thy divine Majesty, and in thy feare and favour, with unfaigned repentance and amendment of life, that I may obtaine thy gracious pardon for all my offences ; and Lord, give me true faith, stedfast hope, and perfect charity unto my lifes

G   end.

end. These great mercies I aske at thy gracious hands, deare Jesus Christ, who art my only Saviour, Redeemer, Mediator, and Advocate; to whom be all praise and glory for ever. Amen.

---

27. *A morning Prayer for Friday, to God the Sonne.*

SWeet Saviour, none can come to the Father but by thee; and whosoever commeth unto thee thou castest not away, but wilt raise him up at the last day unto eternall life.

Now deare Jesus, thou blessed Son, and innocent Lambe of God, that takest away the sinnes of the world, who graciously callest unto thee all heavy laden and penitent sinners that thou maiest ease and refresh them; have pity on me, and vouchsafe to sanctifie and cleanse my soule and body, from all sinne and evill by thy holy Spirit, and make mee pure and upright in thy sight, and be pleased to protect and direct my heart and soule, and all my waies before thee, and to indue me with thy blessed Spirit, to preserve mee from falling into any sin or offence towards thee; but assist me with thy grace in all things I goe about to doe, that I may doe that which may be most acceptable and best pleasing in thy sight. Now Lord, I confesse that I was conceived

ved and borne in finne, and I am a miferable
and wretched finner above all others, and unto
whom fhould I come, but to thee the Saviour of
mankinde, who cameft into the world to fave
finners by thy grace, of whom I am chiefe? O
fountaine of mercy, who didft vouchfafe to bee
borne of the bleffed and pure Virgin *Mary*, (to become man)and tookeft our wretched nature upon
thee, therein to fuffer death, to ~~reaffure~~ us from
eternall death, finne, the grave, hell and Sathan,
and didft willingly lay down thine owne life for
us, which no man could take from thee, that wee
might live by faith through thee; and alfo thou
hadft power to take it up againe, and didft rife
from the grave the third day for our juftification,
and to ~~vanifh~~ all our fpirituall enemies: and laft-
ly, thou our Lord, didft glorioufly afcend into heaven, there to take poffeffion, and make interceffi-
on for us unto thy heavenly Father, with whom
thou doft reigne in heaven for ever, whither thou
doft gracioufly and daily draw to thee all thofe
that truly beleeve in thee, there to live hereafter
with thee; of which number, deare Lord, in the
fulneffe of thy mercies make me one. Now I further humbly pray thee, fweet Jefus, the Saviour
of all that truft in thee, that thou wilt have mercy
on mee, to forgive and pardon all my finnes and
offences paft, and prefent, both originall and a-
ctuall, of omiffion and commiffion, of infirmity
or prefumption, whatfoever I ftand guilty of be-

× ranfome ×   G 2 × vanquifh × fore

fore theee, and even those secret sinnes, that none
but thy All-seeing eyes, and my owne conscience
can testifie against mee, which is more then a
thousand witnesses : I humbly pray thee to cast
them all behinde thy backe into the pit of oblivion, never to come in remembrance with thee;
and wash all my faults out of thy sight with that
blessed streame of thine owne most pretious
blood, which thou didst so plentifully shed for us
in thy most bitter passion. O blessed Lord, let not
all these thy mercies and benefits which thou hast
done and purchased for mankinde, be fruitlesse or
in vaine towards mee, thy poore unworthy servant, whose confidence is only in thee, that thou
wilt make mee a happy partaker of all thy great
benefits and favours : And sweet Iesus, grant
through thy mercies, merits and infinit sufferings,
that my transgressions may never bee laid to my
charge : for there is no other name under heaven
but thine only, blessed Iesus our righteous Lord,
by which we can be saved. To thee bee rendred
as is due all honour, praise, thanks, and glory, for
ever and ever : Concluding my petition with
that perfect Prayer, which thy selfe hast taught
us, saying, *Our Father which art in heaven, &c.*

✗ *meanes on earth nor* ✗

28.   *A*

28. *A Prayer for Friday night, to God the Sonne, our blessed Saviour.*

I Will love thee dearly, O Lord my strength, for thou art my helper, my refuge, and the lifter up of my head, and I will praise thy name so long as I have breath. O Lord Christ, by whom was fulfilled the Law and the Prophets, and in thee all the promises of God are Yea and Amen, to the glory of God the Father, and the comfort of all thy servants; thou art that pure and innocent Lambe of God, that was killed and is alive, to thee was given all power, honour and glory, who liveth and raigneth for ever in heaven and earth, of whose Kingdome there is no end; to thee Lord bee all possible praise and thanks for ever. This is my only Lord and blessed Saviour Jesus Christ the righteous, who died for our sinnes, and rose againe for our justification, and art our Advocate in heaven; so that whatsoever we shall ask the Father in thy name, according to thy will, if we beleeve, we shall obtaine it for thy sake, who art the beloved Son of God, in whom only hee is well pleased. My deare God, have mercy upon me a most grievous sinner to pardon all my offences past, in soule or body, of ignorance or wilfulnesse, of frailty; neglect, contempt or wicked stubbornesse; bury them all, sweet Jesus, in thy grave, and cleanse them from before thine eyes,

G 3　　　　　　　with

with thy most pretious bloud, which thou didst of
thine owne accord and infinite love shed for us, to
free us from eternall death which by our sinnes
are due ; therefore gracious Lord, grant through
thy merits , and manifold sufferings, that my iniquities may never be able to appeare before thee
against me, either to accuse or condemne me, neither in this life, at my death, nor in the great and
last judgement : but in that dreadfull day, Lord by
all thy mercies I beseech thee, shew thy self my loving Saviour, to passe by & cover all my misdeeds
with thy righteousnesse ; that so I may escape thy
just wrath which my transgressions have deserved. Now, deare Iesus, while I live here, make
me thy unworthy servant wholly thine, to be thy
faithfull and constant disciple, and so to love thee
as to keep thy Commandements which are not
grievous, but in obeying them there is great reward ; and let me so follow thee here, as to bee
lowly and meek , to forsake my selfe and the
world, and to take up all my crosses with patience,
and strive to goe after thy steps, though I be farre
unable to drinke of that heavy and bitter cup of
Gods wrath of which thou so deeply tastedst, who
art the propitiation for our sinnes to deliver us
from that fearfull condemnation due unto us : my
offences Lord , I confesse did adde unto that
weighty burden of Gods heavy displeasure , and
our grievous sinnes which thou didst beare upon
the crosse for all true beleevers , who shall passe
from

from death, to life eternall, which thy sufferings, O Chrift, hath purchased for us; whereby I, the unworthieft of thy servants doe also hope to follow thee hereafter, from the grave to heaven, at the refurrection of the juft, that according to thy will declared before thy death; all that are thine fhall bee with thee, even where thou art to enjoy all bliffe and happineffe; in thine owne love by thy unmerited mercies, we fhall bee made partakers with thee of thy heavenly Kingdome of glory, there to ferve and praife thy glorious Name, who art moft worthy, world without end. Amen.

---

29. *The conclufion for Friday night.*

LOrd Iefus, vouchfafe to receive me this night into thy gracious protection both in life and death: And deare Lord, I humbly pray thee to inlighten me with thy grace rightly and faithfully to ferve and obey thee in all true devotion; and with due fubmiffion to thy holy will in all things fo long as I live; and now Lord, I am in health laid downe in my bed by thy loving permiffion, hoping to take quiet reft and fleep, which I befeech thee to give me, and alfo I truft by thy mercie to awake in thy grace and favour to the morning light againe; becaufe thou gracious Lord,

G 4   doft

doſt only me ſuſtaine, and wilt in ſafety thy poore
ſervant keep ; who doe moſt humbly commend
and commit my ſelfe, my ſoule and body, my
children and grand-children, and all I have to
thee, from whom I have received all the good I
doe enjoy, for thou haſt ſhewed great mercies
unto me ; for which I bleſſe and praiſe thy holy
Name, beſeeching thee to give me grace, never
to forget thy benefits, but to continue Lord thy
true and faithfull ſervant unto my death, and for
ever. Amen.

---

30. *A Prayer to the bleſſed Trinity, at firſt waking for Saturday morning.*

I Will praiſe the Lord becauſe he is good, for his
mercy endureth for ever ; by whom we live,
move, and have our being, our maintenance, ſafety and preſervation. Now glorious Trinity, Father, Son, and Holy Ghoſt, I humbly pray thee,
vouchſafe unto mee thy moſt unworthy ſervant,
ſuch grace and favour to, knit my heart and ſoule
faſt to theee, ſo that my ſinnes, nor my ſoules enemies, the wicked world, my owne corrupt fleſh,
nor the malice of the Divell, may not be able to
pluck mee out of thy mercifull and powerfull
hands ; but Lord aſſiſt me with thine owne bleſſed Spirit, that I may daily continue and increaſe
floly   in

in all sincere and perfect love and obedience towards thy Majesty, and in thy feare and favour, and all other saving graces, to have a good conscience before thee, with true faith, stedfast hope, and perfect charity unto my lifes end. Amen.

---

31. *A Prayer unto the Trinity for Saturday morning.*

O Lord our God, how excellent is thy Name in all the world, for thou hast laid the foundation of the earth, and the heavens are the workes of thy hands, and thou didst create, and dost governe, dispose and rule the whole world, with all things therein, according to thy good pleasure. O most divine and adored Trinity, Father Son and Holy Ghost, three persons, but one true, eternall and everliving God, to whom be all praise, honour and glory as is right and due for ever. Thou only by thy word and power didst make all things for thine owne glory; especially mankinde after thine image in purity and holinesse to thine own service; for by thy providence and mercy commeth all good gifts and blessings unto us, and also deliverances only from thee, of those evills and dangers which sinne hath made us subject unto in falling from thee, and our first integrity, by the subtillity and malice of Sathan and

our

our owne frailty, yet of thine owne free grace thou didst elect a number by thee selected of thy chosen servants to inherit an eternall Kingdome, with and through thy beloved Son, whom thou didst ordain and send into the world at thine appointed time to be the redemption of all that beleeve in thee. O God the Son our blessed Lord Jesus Christ, it is written of thee that thou shouldest doe the will of God the Father, who ordained thee to be our Redeemer, and wert made of God unto us, wisdome, righteousnesse, sanctification and salvation, with glorification hereafter. Now deare Jesus, who hast paid our ransome, even the all-sufficient and acceptable sacrifice of thine own pretious bloud to wash away our sins, who was lifted upon the crosse between heaven and earth to make an attonement betwixt God and man, his heavy wrath and our grievous offences, and so thou art become our Priest, to offer up thy innocent selfe to cleanse us from our sinnes, who art our Prophet to instruct and teach us and direct our waies aright, to shew us the path of life, and make the way plaine before our faces, and by thy example, to beare our crosse patiently, and follow thee that art the way, the truth and the life, to lead us to eternall salvation; also thou art our King to protect, defend, and reigne over us in mercy, truth and righteousnesse, till thine enemies be made thy footstoole, and all that hate thee be destroyed before thee, for God hath

put

put all things in fubjection under his feet, then
fhalt thou judge the whole world in righteoufneffe and equity, and wilt bring thy fervants, to
that eternall inheritance, which thou haft by thy
merits and fufferings fo dearly purchafed for us,
who wert borne unto us to be the joy and comfort of all people, and the glory and falvation of
all that truly beleeve and truft in thee our Saviour.
O God Holy Ghoft, the giver, worker and fealer
of all graces unto us; by thee we are called to
the knowledge of God and his faving truth, fanctified to the performance of his will and Commandements certified by the holy Spirit of our
falvation in Chrift Jefus, and by thee applied unto
us to bee regenerated and borne againe by thy
holy operation from fin to grace, to thy glory and
our endleffe felicity. And thy Spirit alfo witnef-
feth to our fpirits that we are the children of God
and heires with Chrift of the Kingdome of heaven to the eternall comfort of all thy fervants, being by thee alfo united to our bleffed Chrift, and
fealed to the day of redemption, and continually
affifting us to all goodneffe. Now great and
glorious Lord God, Father, Son, and Holy Ghoft,
thou haft plentifully powred downe thy manifold
mercies and favours upon us; and multiplied exceedingly thy bleffings and benefits fpirituall and
temporall towards us before we had being in the
world, fince we were borne, and after death thou
haft laid up an eternall weight of glory for all
those

those to possesse that truly beleeve in thee, which give me grace to doe, for none hath or ever can deserve them.   Oh the abundant mercy, bounty, and goodnesse of our gracious God towards mortall mankinde ! who can declare the height and depth of Gods unspeakable love, or be sufficiently thankfull to him for such unexpressible benefits; but with *David*, we may say (Lord) What is man that thou art mindefull of him ?   Or what shall we render to thee for all thy mercies, having in us no good at all ; but what wo receive from thy selfe?, therefore Lord, adde this further grace unto thy former favours, by the assistance of thine owne Spirit , to make us thy unworthy servants, able, rightly, faithfully, and constantly to feare, love, honour, serve, obey and praise thy most glorious Name while we live , and for ever and ever.   Amen.

32. *A Prayer to God the Holy Ghost, for Saturday night.*

O God Holy Ghost, the giver of all graces and and my gracious sanctifier , comforter and preserver, thou knowest my infirmities, my inclination to all evill , and backwardnesse to any goodnesse : vouchsafe Lord, to sanctifie mee thy poore sinfull servant, in soule, body and spirit

through-

throughout, to thy true feare, intire love, and right faithfull and conftant fervice, all my time to come : And be pleafed Lord, by thy grace to enlighten my dull foule and underftanding, with the found knowledge, fincere love, and ftedfaft beleefe of thy faving truth, and keepe me ever conftant therein. And vouchfafe, deare Lord, to inrich me thy poore unworthy fervant, with the infinite treafure of that heavenly wifdome from above,which waiteth about thy Throne, that may teach me thy holy will, and what is good and acceptable unto thee ; and inable me with grace to doe it, that fo I may difcerne between good and evill, and make me fhunne and hate that which is evill, and follow and cleave unto that which is good ; and to withdraw my love from this vaine world, and fix my affections upon thee my God, and on heavenly things that are above, that my chiefe treafure may be fettled there in heaven,and my heart alfo : and fo I fhall firft feek to obtaine that which is moft needfull, even thy glory, thy favour, and thy bleffed Kingdome, and then Lord, I know thou wilt fupply all the defects of grace in my foule, and heale all the infirmities of my body; but chiefly vouchfafe daily to continue and increafe all fpirituall graces in my foule by thy mercy and mighty power, O my bleffed Lord God : to which end, O gracious Spirit, give mee an upright and penitent heart, an humble and lowly fpirit, a quiet recollected minde, freed

and to do thy good from

from the vanities and cares of this present world, and the love of this vile life; but Lord teach mee with *Mary* first and above all things to seek after thee my God, thy Kingdome, and the righteousnesse thereof, so that I may have grace wholly to devote and dedicate my selfe, my time and best endeavours unto thy true and faithfull service, and daily study and strive to doe thy holy will in all things, and seek thy glory here, that so I may be partaker of thy heavenly Kingdome hereafter. And deare Lord Holy Ghost, inspire me with thy grace daily to heare and read thy holy and blessed word as I ought to do, and that I may so imploy my time therein as to frame my life hereafter to thy glory and my soules good. And grant mee graciously, O God, to chuse, to speake, and to walke in the waies of truth and righteousnesse, and to set thy heavy judgements against sin continually before my face to deter, and make mee daily to remember my owne last end, and by thy assistance to prepare for it, and to consider the end in all my actions before I doe them, that I may never doe amisse; and let me still remember thy all-seeing eyes are ever upon our waies that I may not displease or offend thee in any thing: But Lord, indue me with thy holy Spirit to direct my heart and all my waies aright before thee, that so thou maiest witnesse to my spirit that I am the childe of God, and ever continue unto mee that unspeakable comfort to give me the joyfull hope

x *nea from all euill* x   of

of my falvation , through my Lord Jefus Chrift,
unto my end : and in my end efpecially eftablifh
me with thy free fpirit to worke in my foul all faving graces that may make me acceptable in thy
fight , through my Lord Jefus Chrift , for whofe
fake I befeech thee further to extend thy goodnes
towards me , to forgive all my finnes and offences that I have done before thee in my whole life
paft, and preferve me in foul and body from all fin
and evill , either committing or falling on mee;
but deare Lord , vouchfafe daily to fupply and be-
ftow upon me all the benefits and bleffings neceffary for this prefent life; but chiefly be pleafed to
fanctifie my foule and body unto thy faithfull fervice, and indue me with all faving graces for my
falvation both in life and death, that fo I may bee
able rightly and conftantly to ferve and pleafe
thee whilft I live here , that alfo by thy gracious
affiftance I may obtaine a *happy* place hereafter to live
with thee eternally , O Holy Ghoft, and my bleffed Lord God, to whom be all thanks and praife
for ever. Amen.

---

33. *The conclufion for Saturday night in bed to
the weeks Prayers for mornings and nights.*

I Moft humbly befeech thee, my Lord God, mercifully to loke upon me and my manifold infirmities,

mities, and for Jesus my Saviours sake, vouchsafe
to forgive and pardon all my sinnes and grievous
offences that I have committed in thy sight all the
daies of my life past; and in thy great mercy turne
from me all those evils that my transgressions have
justly deserved; and Lord, grant me thy preven-
ting grace and fatherly providence to bee still
with mee to preserve me at all times from falling
into any sinne or evill, either to offend thee my
God, or to hurt my owne soule. And vouchsafe,
Lord, so to direct and dispose the heart and waies
of me (thy most unworthy servant) towards
the right performance of all duties and services
that I owe unto thee my God, and the happy ob-
taining (by my Lord Iesus) of everlasting salvation to my owne selfe; that amongst all the
changes, chances and adversities of this miserable,
mutable, and mortall life, I may ever be defen-
ded by thy ready helpe and favour from falling
into sin, shame, harme or danger, either in soule
or body, and may be directed and assisted by thy
grace and providence to walke in the waies of
righteousnesse and true holinesse before thee, that
thou my Lord Holy Ghost, maiest guide me in all
things I goe about, to doe that which may be most
serviceable, acceptable, and best pleasing in the
sight of my Lord God, to whom be all praise, honour, power and eternall glory, for ever and e-
ver. Amen.

The end of the second Book.

written 1638.

This containeth divers Prayers, for

BOOK III.

several occasions, varia requisitt.
Short Prayers which may belong to any the three Books,
when time serves, not for longer devotions.

1. *A short Preface before other prayers or petitions.*

O Lord Holy Ghost, who best knowest my manifold infirmities, have mercy and pity upon me; and vouchsafe to prevent, or to banish and drive away all evill hindrances and temptations that may withdraw my heart from God in the offering up of my prayers and humble petitions unto thy Majesty; and be pleased Lord, to sanctifie, teach and assist me herein with thy holy Spirit and grace, that I may rightly and faithfully performe this duty and service before thee, to thy glory and my good, and comfort of my soule through Christ Jesus. Amen.

2. *A short thanksgiving at first sight of the morning light.*

MY blessed Lord God, I most humbly praise thee for thy gracious preservation of med with quiet rest and health this night past, and bringing
H
ging

ging me in safety to this light; Lord blesse and sanctifie me this day and ever unto thy faithfull service, and keep me alwaies in thy true faith, feare,
favour and ready obedience; and make me constantly and unfaignedly thine all my life time, but
in my death especially, that when it pleaseth thee
to call for me out of this miserable world, thou
maiest bring me to eternall salvation by thine own
merits and meer mercy; sweet Jesus, I most humbly beseech thee. So be it.

3. *A Prayer for helpe in present temptation, in the
time of prayer to our Lord Jesus, who overcame
and subdued the old tempter, the subtile Serpent our
everlasting enemy, from whom God defend us.*

OH my God, heavenly Father, who hast made
and seest all hearts, and knowest my great
affection and fervent desire rightly to serve thee,
and my weaknesse and frailty in performance
thereof, have pity on my infirmities, and assist
me with thy grace. And sweet Jesus my Saviour,
who didst suffer thy selfe to bee tempted by the
Divell, that thou mightest overcome the tempter,
and succour all those that are tempted; to thee
Lord, I call and pray, for helpe and defence a-
gainst this malicious adversary. O God the Holy
Ghost, indue me with thy blessed Spirit and power so to resist him that he may flye from me, and
banish thou Lord, all wicked hindrances and tem-

                                                    ptations

ptations away from thy poore servant in performing all my duties towards thee. Now deare God, have mercy upon me most miserable sinner, and in thy infinite mercy drive away this subtill enemy of my poore soule, with his pernicious agents, the vaine world, and the corruptions of our owne nature, let them not prevaile over me at any time, for these are very ready to assault, tempt and draw my minde from thee in all my devotions, and services that I endeavour to offer unto thy Majesty; and to make my prayers vaine and void, and drive me to fall into wicked neglect towards my God, whereby to prevent, destroy, and divert all my comforts and hopes in thee O Lord, which is the whole life of my soule. But Gracious God, Almighty, whose power and strength is above all, vouchsafe to overcome and banish all from mee, never to returne againe; and let thy blessed Spirit rest constantly in me to withstand all disturbances in the performance of my duty before thee; and deare Lord, make new, cleane, and upright my heart, and frame it to thy holy will, that so by thy gracious assistance, I may faithfully serve and honour thee, please and praise thee my God, now and at all times, in this life and for ever, to thy glory, and my eternall comfort. Amen.

x *auill temptations* x

The

*The afternoone prayers at foure a clock for each day
in the weeke.*

Munday.   1. *A thanksgiving to the blessed Trinity,
Father, Son, and Holy Ghost.*

O My good and gracious God, great and many are thy mercies and blessings I have received from thee both spirituall and temporall,
from time to time; and now what shall I render
unto thee, having no good to returne, but the
poore fruit of my lips, which is nothing unto thee
but the performance of our duties to praise thy
great Name, and to acknowledge all thy benefits?
therefore now I will give thanks to God the Father, our gracious Creator, who so loved us when
we were his enemies, and had lost our selves by
sinne, that he ordained, and after sent his only begotten and beloved Son into the world, that whosoever beleeveth in him should not perish but
have everlasting life; Christ being the propitiation
for our sinnes, that we may live by faith through
him.   And also I yeeld all possible praise unto my
blessed Saviour, who became man, and in his infinite love willingly laid downe his life for us,
and washed away our sinnes with his owne pretious bloud, and made us by his merits and sufferings, Kings and Priests unto God, and adopted
children to his Father, and heires with himselfe of
an eternall Kingdome; by whose resurrection we
have

have a lively hope of an inheritance that cannot be shaken, and withereth not, reserved in heaven for us. Now to thee Lord Holy Ghost, the preserver, sanctifier, and comforter of mankinde, by whom we are sealed unto the day of redemption, and by whose holy working wee are united unto Jesus our blessed head, and are certified by thy Spirit, witnessing to our spirits that wee are the children of God to our great comfort; and further by thy assistance and grace, our weake prayers are rightly and effectually offered up unto the Lord our God. Now to thee, Almighty God, three Persons and glorious Trinity, but one true and everliving God, from whose mercifull hands we daily receive all the good we doe injoy in this present world, with further and full assurance of far greater happinesse by thy infinite mercies in the life to come, be all praise and glory. Amen.

to thy great majesty

Tuesday. 2. A Prayer to the Trinity for grace and true faith.

O Sweet Jesus Christ, Son of God, who art the divine word, without whom nothing was made, and being made had been utterly lost, hadst thou not been our powerfull and mercifull Redeemer; thou art the way, the truth, and the life, and thou who hast said, that no man can come unto the Father but by thee; who camest into the world, and didst willingly lay down thine owne

H 3   life

life only to save sinners by thy grace, of whom I
am chiefe; have mercy upon me miserable sinner,
who can of my selfe neither will nor performe a-
ny good worke towards God as I ought to doe :
but vouchsafe Lord, to indue mee with grace to
serve and obey thee, to learne thy will and to doe
it, and through faith to lay hold of thy mercies,
that so thou my Saviour maiest in thy righteousnesse present me to thy heavenly Father, that hee
may looke upon me poor sinfull creature, through
thee his deare Son, and for thy sake to receive and
accept me into his gracious favour, to pardon all
my sinnes, and save my soule, through thy perfect
righteousnesse, and manifold sufferings all performed for me. Now thou Lord hast further said that
none can come unto thee except the Father draw
him, therefore I most humbly pray thee, O God
the Father, by that infinite love towards mankind,
which caused thee to send downe thy beloved
Son out of thine owne bosome into this wicked
world, that whosoever beleeveth in him should
not perish, but have everlasting life : I earnestly
pray thee, O God the Father, to draw me to thy
Son Jesus, that I may lay fast hold by faith on him
to be my Saviour, and to be his faithfull and constant servant, and to be made through him, and by
thy mercie a happy member of him our blessed
head, & then I shall be sure never to fall into condemnation, but by stedfast faith in him obtaine e-
ternall salvation : And deare Lord Holy Ghost,
the

the giver of grace, by whom we are joyned to
our Lord and head Chrift, and fanctified to a new
and holy life : Lord cleanfe and frame my heart
and foule by the holy working and affiftance of
thy Spirit and grace, unto the right, faithfull and
conftant fervice of my Lord God my Saviour Jefus, with thee O Holy Ghoft, fo long as I live :
Lord daily increafe my faith and all faving graces
in me for my falvation, and may by thee be directed and lead into the waies of righteoufneffe, untill thou haft brought me unto endleffe happineffe
through Jefus Chrift.   Amen.

Wednefday.   3. A prayer to God for charity.

O Mercifull Lord God, the giver of all graces,
I humbly befeech thee to frame my heart,
will and affections, in all ready obedience to thy
moft holy will and Commandements in all things,
efpecially in the workes of mercy, and charity,
they being a fweet fmelling facrifice wherewith
thou art well pleafed ; and wherein we may imitate thee, and fhall thereby gaine the honour to be
made like unto thy felfe, and be knowne to bee
one of thy difciples if we love our brethren as our
felves. O God, as thou haft bleffed mee of thy
meer goodneffe with an eftate above fome others,
fo give me the grace of compaffion and charity,
and inlarge my heart towards thy fervice, to fhew
mercy unto them that want, as thou haft been
                    H 4   merci-

mercifull unto me, that I may willingly diftribute,
communicate to thofe that are in need, and be liberall of my earthly vanifhing wealth to relieve
thy childrens necessities, for thy fake, that are dear
unto thee, who wert free of thy very bloud, and
fparedft not thine owne life to ranfome them and
me from utter deftruction : and fo the loynes and
bellies of the poore fhall praife thee and blefle
me in their comforts; and thou maieft vouchfafe
to receive and accept at my poore hands that
fmall mite of thankfulneffe and obedience towards thee my God, from whofe moft gracious
hand I have received many bountifull bleffings
and benefits throughout my whole life, which let
mee never forget, gratefully to acknowledge
while I have breath, and to praife thy holy Name
for all thy mercies now and for evermore. Amen
deare God. Amen.

Thurfday. 4. *A Prayer to the Trinity for
fpirituall graces.*

MOft gracious Lord God, who didft create
man of the duft of the earth; and knoweft
we are by nature the children of wrath, and wholy
inclined to evill; for thou beft underftandeft how
unapt and unable I finfull creature am to doe any
good before thee, much leffe to call upon thy great
and glorious Name as I ought to doe, yet thou in
mercy haft appointed prayer to bee the chiefe
meanes

meanes betwixt thy great Majesty, and the un-
worthinesse of us thy poore sinfull servants, wher-
by to declare our wants, griefes, and desires unto
thee, who art our only hope and helpe: Therefore
deare Lord, indue me thy unworthy servant with
thy true spirit of grace and prayer, to teach mee
how to pray as I ought, that thereby I may have
power and strength to withstand all evill temptations that seek to draw me from thy service; and
by thy assistance that I may be able so to resist the
Divell that hee may flye from me in the performance of all duties towards thee; and give mee
grace with faith and fervency, humility and true
devotion, to cry and pray daily and constantly
unto thee for relief and distresse in all my troubles
and wants, and faithfully to call and relye upon
thee for all thy blessings and benefits both spirituall and temporall, to be bestowed on my soule
and body as thou shalt thinke fittest; that so I may
render all thanks and magnifie thy Name, as I am
right bound to doe; for all thy mercies and favours vouchsafed unto me the most unworthiest
of all thy servants from time to time. And I humbly pray thee, O Lord, to give me the blessed gift
of true faith, without which it is impossible for
me to please thee my God, that thereby I may lay
hold, and rightly apply unto my owne soule all
the infinite benefits purchased by the bitter death
and passion, and precious bloud-shedding of my
Lord and Saviour Jesus Christ, that I may bring
                                              forth

forth the fruits of righteousnesse and true holinesse
before thee as becommeth that Saints and servants; whereby I may glorifie thee, and have assurance to my owne conscience that I am thine by
constantly obeying thy will: And also Lord grant
me hearty and unfained repentance and true
sorrow for all my sinnes originall and actuall, in
omitting the good I ought to do, and committing
the evill I should not doe against thee, that so I
may obtaine pardon of all my trespasses, through
the merits of Jesus Christ the righteous; and let thy
blessed Spirit produce in me amendment of my
life all my time to come, and assist mee with thy
grace to shun and hate all approaches of evil, and
Lord shew me the way of life, and turne my steps
into the right paths that I may wallke in true obedience to all thy holy Commandements. Now
deare God of thy mercy, give me the true feare of
thy holy Name, with assurance of thy gracious
favour towards me, and continuall joy and comfort in the Holy Ghost, that I may strive alwaies
to keep faith and a good conscience before thee
towards all; and indue me with grace, will, understanding and ability, to do good workes to thy
glory, and bring comfort and profit to my soule in
praying, reading, and hearing of thy most holy
word at all times, and most devout love towards
thy Majesty, with affection to all my brethren, thy
children, servants and all the daies of my life to
come, by thy gracious assistance dear God, Amen.

to thee

Friday.

Friday. 5. *A Prayer for defence against our soules enemies, in all temptations.*

GOod Lord God, who knowest the power and great malice of our spirituall enemies, from who none can defend or deliver us, but only thou, O Lord, whose power and strength is over and above all; and if thou please to receive me into thy gracious protection, who can hurt or plucke mee out of thy mercifull hands? Therefore I most humbly beseech thee, O God, to defend me both in soule and body, in life and death, from all the temptations of my owne wretched nature within me, the wicked inticements of this vaine world round about me, with the malicious snares, and evill temptations of the Divell that are ever at my backe ready to intrap me, and draw my soul from thee my God and all goodnesse, and to lead mee captive into all wickednesse, sinne and evill, to seperate me from thee, all which like roaring Lions seeke to devoure and destroy me everlastingly. But I most humbly pray unto thee, O Lord, who understandest my frailties, to preserve and deliver me from all their assaults, that they may never be able to prevaile over me to draw mee to sin against thee my God, in any thing; neither suffer them to prevent, hinder, disturbe or carry away my minde, or possesse my vaine heart with wandring thoughts in the performance of any holy duty

duty or service towards thy Majesty; nor give them power to bring those harmes, dangers or mischiefes upon me either in soule or body which they desire to doe. But let thy blessed Spirit so fully possesse me, and ever direct and assist mee in all my waies, to doe all things in a right, faithfull and acceptable manner before thee, that so at all times thy Spirit may witnesse unto my spirit, that I am thy childe and servant; and of thy infinite mercy good Lord, vouchsafe thou alwaies to say unto my soule, especially at my death, that thou art my God, my helpe and my salvation for ever: and by thy grace make my heart and soule to answer and performe unto thee againe, that I am, and will bee thy true, faithfull and obedient servant unto my last breath for ever. Amen.

Saturday. 6. A Prayer for the true spirit of prayer, or a meditation. With a short prayer to Jesus our Saviour.

DEare Lord Holy Ghost, the helper of our infirmities, the preserver and sanctifier of mankinde; I most humbly begge of thee to indue mee thy unworthy sinfull servant, with thy true Spirit of grace and prayer, that I may rightly performe that duty towards thee of calling upon thy holy Name, and all other thy service this day and at all times, with true and right devotion, that so my petitions being humbly presented to thy great

Majesty

Majesty lowly and meekly on the knees of my heart & body; they may by thy mercifull assistance be lifted up and ascend by the wings of faith and devotion unto the highest heavens; and there with confidence through my Saviour Jesus, enter into the glorious eares and presence of Almighty God, where all mercy, grace and goodnesse aboundeth. And then my supplications by thy favour, may be heard and accepted by thee my God, to prevaile and draw downe from thy mercifull hand all graces and blessings needfull, upon me thy poore creature both in soule and body; and so my unworthy sacrifice of due praise and thanks that I offer unto thee may be received and accepted by thee, the Lord of all mercies, who doth often take in good part even the will for the deed, from thy fraile unworthy servants, and then my poore prayers shall bring much joy and comfort to me, and give glory to thee, my Lord. To whom (as of right belongs) be all honour and praise, for evermore. Amen.

A short Prayer to our blessed Saviour Jesus, to be joyned to the former prayers.

OH my deare Lord Jesus, who didst in thy infinite mercy give thy innocent selfe to death for me a poore miserable sinner; Lord by thy grace make me to dedicate and offer up my selfe a living sacrifice holy and acceptable unto thee, in

daily

daily striving rightly and faithfully to serve and obey thee, that I may be wholly thine; and as thou hast bought me with an unvaluable treasure, even thine owne most pretious bloud, so sweet Jesus by thy holy Spirit unite me unseparably unto thee, my blessed head; and by thy assistance, that I may become a new creature, to hate and forsake all sinnes, the vaine world, and my wicked selfe, and to be a true, carefull and constant servant unto thee, to feare, love, honour, and glorifie thy great and heavenly Name, who art the comfort and salvation of all that beleeve and trust in thee, which Lord, let me unfaignedly doe, so long as I live.

For y[e] Saboth day (at night.)

7. *A Prayer to God, the Lord of all grace and mercie, containing seven humble petitions from a penitent sinner: 1. For true faith. 2. For the Holy Ghost. 3. For wisdome. 4. For the feare of God. 5. For the love of God, and charity to our neighbours. 6. For repentance and true contrition of heart. 7. And for the grace and right spirit of prayer.*

O Most bountifull Lord God, which giveth to all men liberally, and reproacheth none, if we aske in faith and waver not: and our blessed Saviour maketh us a large promise, saying, Aske and yee shall receive, seeke and you shall finde, knock and it shall bee opened unto you: And whatsoever you shall aske in my Name I will doe
it,

it , if you beleeve when you pray that you fhall
have it ; for your heavenly Father if you aske in
my name , will give the Holy Ghoft to them that
defire him, and wifdome to fuch as aske it of God;
and no good thing fhall be wanting or with-held
from them which feare the Lord, and walke up-
rightly in his fight ; fo that we may well fay with
David, What is man that thou Lord art mindefull
of him , and doft vifit him with thy mercie , and
crowneft him with glory and honour? Moft mercifull Lord, thefe thy gracious promifes and great
goodnefle towards mortall man, imboldneth mee,
though a miferable finner, and moft unworthy of
thy favours, now to offer up my fupplications, and
become an humble futer to thy Majefty, to begge
thefe great bleffings at thy hands, who have juftly
deferved grievous punifhments from thee for my
offences. But of thine owne meer mercie, deare
God , who defireft not the death of a finner, but
our repentance, converfion, and falvation ; and
for thy beft beloved Sons fake, in whom thou wilt
deny us nothing, vouchfafe to incline thine ear to
receive the humble petitions of me thy poore fervant, who prefumeth to crave of thee, the Father
of mercie , and the originall of all goodneffe,
from whom only commeth all good and perfect
gifts; the feven fpirituall and heavenly graces,
wherewith to vanquifh and banifh us from the feven dangerous deadly finnes, which like Serpents
flay and deftroy fo many foules , the leaft finne
we

we commit, being sufficient to condemne us for
ever.   And now first, Good God, I humbly pray
1. thee to bestow upon mee the blessed and most
needfull gift of true faith, without which it is impossible to please thee, whereby I may stedfastly
beleeve and trust in thy goodnesse, and lay fast
hold of all thy mercies and gracious promises, especially upon the merits and sufferings of thy dear
Son, and my Saviour Jesus for my redemption,
and by thy grace rightly to apply them all to my
salvation.   And grant I may with thy assistance,
bring forth such fruits of true holinesse and righteousnesse, as may be most to thy glory and the
peace and comfort of mine owne conscience.
And since I have begun to speake to thee, O Lord,
who am but dust and ashes, vouchsafe for Jesus
2. sake, further to give me the most excellent gift of
the Holy Ghost, to unite me inseparably to my
blessed head and Saviour Christ, and inspire my
soule with all saving graces, which may change
all the evill in me to goodnesse, darknesse to light,
vices to vertues, and so wholy to cleanse and sanctifie my soule, body, and spirit, throughout, that I
may be made perfect to every good worke, and renewed and inabled to all obedience, godlinesse
and holinesse of life before thee :   and I also most
3. humbly beseech thee (O gracious God) to inrich
me thy poore unworthy servant, with the unvaluable treasure of that heavenly wisdome from a-
bove, which abideth about thy Throne, to direct
and

and reforme my heart, and all my wayes aright
in thy fight, and to teach me thy holy will, and
what is good and acceptable unto thee, and inable me with grace to doe it; and likewise Lord
indue me with the true underftanding of thy holy
Lawes, that I may keepe them with my whole
heart unto my end? Now, O my Lord, we are
taught by *Solomon*, That the beginning of wifdome is the feare of the Lord, and the knowledge
of divine things, true underftanding; therefore I
doe moft humbly intreat thee to knit my rebelli-
ous heart to the holy feare of thy glorious Name,
who only art to be feared, with the due confide-
ration of thy righteous and terrible judgements,
who canft caft both body and foul into hel; let this
detaine me from falling into any evill or offence
towards thee, and thereby alfo draw my finfull
foule unto thy faithfull fervice, with true contrition for all my paft tranfgreffions againft thee.
But efpecially, good God, be pleafed to indue my
poore foule with the infinite gift and bleffing of
thy fincere and perfect love of thy divine and
heavenly Majefty who art the true and only good.
And, O God, grant that I may love and honour
thee above and beyond all other things, with all
my heart, all my foule, all my ftrength, and with
all my minde, fetting my affections not on things
that are below, but upon heavenly treafures that
are above, which are permanent and fade not,
where my fweet Saviour who dyed for mee on

I   earth,

earth, now liveth and reigneth with thee in heaven for ever, and maketh intercession for mee
there, that by thy assistance I may continually
study and strive, carefully and willingly to performe all duties towards thee in obeying thy
Commandements with an upright and perfect
heart before thee : and in all true charity being
ready to doe good to others as thou commandest,
and to love my neighbour as my selfe, even my e-
nemies for thy sake. Most mercifull Lord, who
knowest our fraile and wretched natures, and desirest the conversion, & not the confusion of poor
miserable sinners; thou sweet Jesus, camest to call,
not the righteous, but sinners to repentance, such
as I am, and to save that which was lost ; Oh let
not my poore soule be lost which cost thee thy
deare pretious bloud to save; but Lord, make mee
by true faith lay hold of my redemption by thee,
and all other thy workes of mercy; and though I
have grievously offended in thy sight, yet I beseech
thee, with-hold not thy favour from me thy poor
sinfull servant, but give me the grace of unfeigned
sorrow and repentance, with a true contrite spirit, and a broken heart for all my sinnes committed before thee, from the greatest to the least,
wherein I have displeased thee, by thought, desire,
word or deed; hating, judging and condemning
my selfe, for so offending thee my Lord God; and
most earnestly and humbly crave thy assistance,
that I may now happily returne to thee with a

penitent

penitent and grieved heart, from whom I have
so unhappily gone astray by a vaine corrupt mind
and sinfull soule, whereby I hope in thy great
mercy to escape thy just wrath and condemnation due to my grievous offences; and may also obtaine thy gracious pardon for all my passed misdeeds, with the assistance of thy holy Spirit,
which I most humbly crave, to amend my former
faults, and to reforme my wayes the rest of my
life in all things according to thy blessed will.
Now lastly, O gracious Lord our righteousnesse,
my sure hope and heavenly Father, the fountaine
of all goodnesse, in whom is all mercy and compassion, from thee only we receive all good gifts
and graces; for thou hearest the prayers, and to
thee shall all flesh come, who understandest our
wants before we aske, and knowest our wretched
natures and disabilities to all goodnesse, so that
thy grace only must worke both the will and the
deed of all that is good in us, and then of thine
owne mercie accept the same through the merits
and mediation of our Saviour Jesus; so doubling
thy favours towards us miserable mortall creatures, whose hearts are vile and false unto our
selves and to thee also, and our thoughts are only
evill continually : Therefore sweet Jesus the mirrour of mercie, vouchsafe to heare and helpe me,
to call and draw me to thy selfe, and knit fast my
heart and soule unto thy true feare, devout love,
and faithfull service for ever; that so by thy selfe,

I may be inabled to run willingly and joyfully after thee, rightly and readily to performe all duties
towards thee, and keep all thy Commandements
constantly.   Oh gracious Lord Holy Ghost, our
blessed preserver, comforter and sanctifier, sof-
ten thou my hardened heart by thy grace, and inlighten my dull and sinfull soule, with all the powers thereof, my understanding, memory, will
and affection, with all saving graces; especially
as the chiefe means to gaine the rest, vouchsafe to
inspire me with thy true spirit of grace and prayer
rightly, humbly, fervently and faithfully to call
daily on thy sacred Name, and to worship thee
in spirit and truth, even as thou requirest to be served, that so by thy favour I may obtaine grace,
power and strength, to banish all wandring
thoughts, and to vanquish and resist all wicked
hindrances cast in by the divell or his agents, the
world, and mine owne corruptions, which di-
stract and disturbe my serious and devout atten-
dance of both soule and body in rightly performing this duty of prayer unto my Lord God,
whereby I may be duly thankfull for all thy benefits and mercies, already bestowed on me and
mine, and also to begge and obtaine the gracious
countenance of all thy blessings spirituall and temporall, in whatsoever thou seest necessary for this
present life, and that which is to come; but more
especially in giving me all saving graces, which
may fit, prepare and further me here for thy hea-
x continuance x   venly

venly Kingdome hereafter. To which my Saviour and Redeemer bring me by all the merits and sufferings, and in the fulnesse of thy mercies, I humbly beseech thee, dear Jesus. Amen, Amen.

1. *A sorrowfull widowes prayer and petition unto the gracious protector and defender of widowes, and father of the fatherlesse, which I composed shortly after the death of my dear husband: And this may also serve any other upon the like occasion.*

ALmighty God, and most gracious Lord, who art full of pity and goodnesse, vouchsafe to heare, assist, and accept the humble devotion and supplication of me thy poore unworthy servant, in Jesus Christ thy deare Son. Most mighty God, whose mercies are above all thy great works, and whose power and divine providence directeth and disposeth all things to the best, for those that doe love and depend upon thee. Thou hast ever been pleased to shew mercie unto me thy poore handmaid, the most sinfull of all thy servants, and hast taken care of mee even from my mothers wombe, and vouchsafed me many benefits and blessings, and delivering mee out of very great crosses and troubles, still holding me up by thy gracious hand from sinking in the midst of a sea of sorrowes; and like a most loving Father in my divers change of fortunes, hast at all times provided for me and mine beyond our deserts, or the

I 3   worlds

worlds expectation, having in thy mercifull goodnesse made me see with comfort all my children, who were left destitute, now by thy provident provision and blessing, well setled for this life : All which by thy infinite favours, Lord make me ever thankfully to acknowledge, and grant that I and all mine, may serve, obey, praise, and glorisie thy great and blessed Name for ever, and ever. And as thou Lord, hast stretched forth thy hand of bounty to supply all my worldly wants; so dear God, vouchsafe more especially to extend thy gracious care over my soule, to prevent and keep me from sin, and indue me with all spirituall graces, so that my whole life and waies may ever be serviceable and acceptable to thy heavenly Majesty. And now, O Lord, since it hath been thy will and pleasure, to take away, and call to thy selfe my deare husband out of this transitory life before me, and to bereave me of him who was my chiefe comfort in this world : I humbly beseech thee, vouchsafe to take me into thy care, and give me grace to choose with *Mary* that better part which may never be taken from mee, chiefly to serve and follow thee, that so I may turne this freedome from the bond of mariage only the more to thy service, and may become thy bondwoman to serve and praise thee day and night like *Hanna*, so long as I live. And Lord, assist me with thy grace to obey thee in all things according to thy holy will, daily endeavouring to

work

work out my falvation with feare and trembling, and continually ſtriving by a godly life and holy converſation, to make my calling and election ſure, which is one of the chiefeſt things needfull. Now deare God, make me to change and far exceed the fervent affection and carefull obſervance I have lived in towards my husband, into a holy feare, with devout and ſincere love of thy Majeſty and ſervice, and due watchfulneſſe over my ſelfe, that I diſpleaſe not thee my God in any thing. And good God, by thy holy Spirit, withdraw my heart from the covetous ſeeking, deſiring and longing after the vanities, riches, delights, preferments, or vaine pleaſures of this wicked deceitfull world, but inſtead of my former care and troubles in worldly buſineſſes, to pleaſe my husband, and for the good of my children, let me now bend my minde, and wholly ſet my heart and ſoule, to ſeeke after thee my good God, thy glory, thy Kingdome, and the righteouſneſſe thereof, that ſo I may walke before thee all the reſt of my daies, with an upright, faithfull, and perfect heart in thy ſight. Laſtly, indue mee with true thankfulneſſe to thy gracious Majeſty for all thy manifold mercies vouchſafed unto me, Lord give me grace to uſe thoſe benefits thou beſtoweſt on me conſcionably as may be beſt pleaſing unto thee, and to imploy all I have to thy glory, the relievement of thy trueſt ſervants, and my owne comfort, eſpecially the good of my

I 4   ſoule

soule in performing my duty towards thee, in striving to doe all the good I can, while I have time,
for I desire so to use and receive thy blessings
here, as I may be also received into the place of
eternall blessednesse hereafter, through Jesus
Christ my Lord. Finally, I most humbly beg that
thou wilt vouchsafe to be a loving and gracious
Father in thy care and comfort to me, and all
mine, and let thy mercie, blessing and favour, rest
alwaies upon me, my children and grand-children
kindred and friends, with all that thou hast given
thy poore servant, who doth in all humility
commend and commit my selfe, my waies and
workes, wholy to thy most blessed protection,
and direction, to dispose according to thy good
pleasure; that so I may doe all things to thy glory
here, and by thy mercy be a happy partaker of thy
eternall Kingdome of glory hereafter, through
Jesus Christ my Lord, Amen.

2. *A Prayer to the God of mercy in time of affliction.*

O Most gracious Lord God, the originall of all
goodnesse, and fountaine of mercie, thou
hast commanded thy poore servants to call upon
thee in the day of trouble, that thou maiest deliver us, and we may glorifie thee; great are the
troubles of thy children, but thou deliverest them
out of all; thine eyes, O Lord, are upon thy servants

vants, and thine eares are open to their cry, for
thou art near unto all that call upon thee in truth,
and wilt save such as bee afflicted in spirit : the
sorrows of my heart are increased, Lord draw me
out of my troubles; the poore crieth, and the Lord
heareth, he prepareth their hearts, and bendeth
his eares to them, and delivereth them out of all
their feare and care : for the hope afflicted, shall
not perish before thee for ever. The Lord also
will be a refuge in due time, even in affliction,
and they that know thy Name will trust in thee,
for thou wilt not faile them that seek thee : have
mercy upon me, O Lord, consider my troubles
which I suffer of them that hate me without cause,
thou hast been my defence, and hast lifted me up
from the gates of death : O Lord my God, in thee
I put my trust, save me from them that persecute
mee, and deliver me in thy good time. But, dear
God, I most humbly confesse that my sinnes are
so many and grievous, as they have deserved farre
greater punishment then I am able to beare, and
I can hope for no helpe or releasebut from thine
owne goodnesse, who art my only hope and sure
refuge ; for thou hast mercy on whom thou wilt
have mercy, and takest compassion on whom
thou pleasest; but I acknowledge that my sufferings
are not answerable to my sinnes, for thou hast
corrected me with favour, not in rigor; therefore
if thou shouldest kill me, yet will I trust in thee,
for thy mercy exceedeth all thy workes, and under

derthe shadow of thy wings will I rest in confidence, till all my afflictions be overpassed. Yet Lord, if it seem good unto thee to continue these heavy troubles and visitations, that now lye sore on me, I humbly pray thee to sanctifie all my afflictions unto me thy poore servant, which I hope are but fatherly chastisements for the amendment of my faults, and not the fearfull judgements and ensignes of thy wrathfull displeasure; from which Lord, for thy Sonnes sake, preserve me thy poore sinfull creature, and lay no more upon me then thou wilt make me able to undergoe as I ought to doe, saying with *Ely*, It is the Lord, let him do what he pleaseth: and make me to consider like *Job*, that naked I came into the world, and naked I shall returne, the Lord gave, and the Lord hath taken, praised be his name for ever; but thou Lord art my stength and my stay in all distractions. I further humbly beseech thee, to give me grace and patience in all things, and at all times, to keep my selfe from any offence towards thee, by repining at thy just and favourable corrections for my transgressions; but grant that I may as Christ hath taught us, meekly and humbly, submit my selfe to thy most righteous and blessed will, that so I may (by thy assistance) make the best and right use of whatsoever thou sendest, that all may be to the best for thy honour, and turne to my good when thou art pleased to give a happy issue to this temptation, and in thy good time to ease and deliver

liver me out of these great adversities to thy glory.
But I know that the afflictions of this present
world, are not worthy of the glory that shall bee
revealed to us hereafter ; yet I humbly desire if it
so please thee, that I may live the rest of my daies
in peace and quiet , constantly to attend thy service, and seek after my owne salvation. Lord be
mercifull to this whole Kingdome , now in very
great distraction, distresse and misery, and also to
all my fellow members in thy whole Church uni-
versall , wheresoever any of us are afflicted , inwardly or outwardly in body or minde , grant us
either speedy delivery , or else grace to performe
thy good pleasure, and with patience to wait thy
leasure , untill thou please to have mercy on us to
our release and comfort , and to thy owne praise
and glory , who never failest those that depend
upon thee. Now I most humbly acknowledge
with all possible praise and thanks , which I am
bound ever to render unto thee, that thou hast formerly delivered me out of many sorrowes , cares,
troubles and vexations , both in body and minde,
and also I blesse and magnifie thy holy Name for
all thy great and manifold blessings which thou
hast bestowed upon me , thy most unworthy servant ; and I pray thee Lord, of thy infinite goodnesse , not to let my sinnes and wickednesse hinder thy mercies towards me, but pardon and cast
all my offences out of thy sight , through Jesus
Christ my Saviour, and vouchsafe alwaies to con-

tinue

tinue thy grace and favour to mee, and especially
in daily renewing all spirituall graces in me, that
so, when, or how soone soever thou hast appointed an end unto my daies here , I may then obtaine the end of my faith and hope, even thy glory
and my owne salvation, through thy beloved Son
and my only Saviour Jesus : for whose sake, Lord
heare me, and grant these my humble requests, with
all things else which thou best knowest necessary
either for my soule or body, for this life, or for the
life to come, in which, deare God, make thee in
thy manifold mercies partaker of eternall happinesse for evermore.   Amen.

3. *A Prayer for due preparation before the holy Communion of the Lords Supper.*

O Most gracious God , and our heavenly and
    mercifull Father in Jesus Christ, who hatest
nothing thou hast made, and desirest not the
death of sinners, but that we should return to thee
and live; thou absolvest all those that truly repent
and beleeve thy holy Gospell, and didst send thine
only and beloved Son Jesus into the world , to
seek those that were lost , and to save sinners by
thy grace, of whom I am chiefe. O sweet Jesus,
thou callest to thee , those that are heavy laden
and truly penitent , and weary of their burthen-
some sinnes , that thou maiest mercifully ease and
refresh them; thou camest to call sinners to repentance,

tance, and reſtore us that were loſt by ſinne, and
to lay downe thine owne life to redeeme mankinde from eternall death, and haſt left us a gracious remembrance thereof in thy moſt holy Supper
of that unſpeakable worke of our redemption,
which we are exceedingly bound often to celebrate, in acknowledgement of thy unexpreſſible
mercy and favour towards us. But oh my Lord!
I tremble and feare, knowing that I am a wretched and wicked ſinner, and my offences have
made me abominable in thy ſight, being wholy
corrupt both in ſoule and body, from the crowne
of my head, to the ſoal of the foot, the worſt de-
ſerving of all thy ſervants, and if thou ſhouldeſt
ſtrictly marke what I have done amiſſe, or enter
into judgement with me, how ſhould I dare to
come into thy preſence having nothing to anſwer
for my ſelfe, but (to cry with the Publican) I have
grievouſly offended; Lord be mercifull to mee a
ſinner? (and as another ſaith of himſelfe, how
ſhould I preſume to appeare in the preſence of
God, can the Lord be mercifull to ſo miſerable a
ſinner as I am?) But Lord, I have learned, and do
beleeve that there is mercy with thee, and plentifull redemption; therefore we are infinitly bound
to love and feare thee; but I doe humbly confeſſe
that I am altogether unworthy of my ſelfe to approach unto thy bleſſed table, but thou Lord that
giveſt both the will and the deed in all good
workes, ſo Lord I pray thee to worke in me a due
                                              pre-

preparation for thy acceptance, and then inable me to performe my duty herein in a right and faithfull manner, for there at thy heavenly banquet, thou Lord, Father, Son and Holy Ghost, art present in thy great Majesty beholding our unperfect devotions, wants in preparation, and manifold infirmities; but thou Lord by thy powerfull grace cleansest us from sin, and changest us into new creatures, and in thy highest bounty giving thy selfe really unto us to be received spiritually by faith, and by the working of the Holy Ghost; thou art the heavenly food of our soules unto eternall life, powring such great and wonderfull treasure into poore earthen vessels, as we are, and and so making us partakers of all the benefits of thy unspeakable merits, and bitter passions and sufferings. Oh Lord, who invitest me thither, continue thy mercy to perfect the good worke thou hast begun for my salvation, and heale thou my corrupt soule, converting my straying and deceitfull heart, and knit it unto thee my God, and by thy grace prepare and fit me, rightly, reverently, faithfully and worthily, to receive that high and divine mystery, in all humility, contrition, true faith and charity, with such devotion as I ought to doe. Now deare Lord, give me grace rightly to understand, and duly to consider and ponder of thy greatnesse to feare thee, of thy goodnesse to love thee, of thy power and manifold mercies towards me, ever to beleeve and trust

in

in thee : And alfo to looke into my owne rebelli-
ous difobedience, and fhamefull ingratitude towards thee, and my moft miferable eftate, who
am in danger of everlafting damnation by my innumerable tranfgreffions committed againft thee;
Lord touch my hardened heart with the oyle of
thy grace, that it may be faftened to receive a
found and fenfible feeling and fight of all my grie-
vious finnes paft, both in committing the evill I
was forbidden, and omitting the good I am commanded, with a true fenfe of thy juft wrath a-
gainft me for the fame, which may worke in mee
by thy affiftance, fuch unfaigned forrow and pe-
nitencie, even to breake my ftony heart with hatred of my felf and all finne for fo offending thee,
with fuch true contrition and repentance unto falvation, as I may obtaine thy mercifull pardon fweet Jefus, that by thy wounds I may bee
healed, and all my offences hidden, never to bee
imputed unto me hereafter; and by thy grace heartily purpofing, conftantly to endeavour the a-
mendment of all my mifdeeds for the time to
come, and by thy helpe to lead a holy and a fanctified life fo long as I live. Now I humbly befeech thee, oh dear Lord, to indue me alfo with
the bleffed gift of true faith, which is the only
hand to lay hold of thee, and all thy mercies
whereby thou maieft dwell in me, and I in thee
for ever; I beleeve, Lord helpe my unbeleefe,
and ftrengthen and increafe in me a right hope,

and lively faith, ftedfaftly to beleeve , and rightly
to apply to my owne foule all thy gracious promifes, benefits, merits and fufferings for me to my
falvation. Oh my God Holy Ghoft, vouchfafe to
infpire my heart with true and perfect charity towards all my brethren and neighbours, yea even
to my very enemies for thy fake , that I may forgive them, as thou doft pardon me.   And thou
Lord, preferver of mankinde, by thy gracious o-
peration in this bleffed Sacrament , joyne me an
unworthy member unfeparably unto thy bleffed
head Chrift Jefus, efpecially at this time, grant that
through thy holy working and affiftance , I may
bee a happy partaker not only of the outward
fignes, but alfo of the inward and ineftimable graces beftowed upon our foules by the reall body
broken, and pretious bloud fhed of our deare Saviour Jefus, which was crucified for us, to be the
pretious food of our foules, all which Lord rightly
apply unto my foule, with all other benefits thereby fignified and affured unto us , and through his
righteoufneffe and merits, that I may be reconciled and accepted by God our heavenly Father, to
my eternall comfort and happineffe; that fo I may
devoutly and everlaftingly love and honour,
magnifie, and admire the infinite mercy, love and
favour of God , the Father, our deare Saviour Jefus, and of the Holy Ghoft, to whom be all praife
and glory for ever.   Now Almighty God, grant
me thy poore fervant grace to live in true faith,
                                                      ready

ready obedience, and continuall thankfullnesse all the rest of my daies here, that I may live hereafter in heaven with thee, in joy and blisse for evermore. Amen.

4. *An humble thanksgiving after the receiving of the Sacrament of the Lords Supper.*

I Yeeld unto thee my mercifull Lord God, Father, Son and Holy Ghost, all humble and possible praise and thanks, for all thy great benefits and loving favours vouchsafed unto me, thy poor sinfull creature both spirituall and temporall all my life hitherto; and deare Lord, the fountaine of all mercie, thou hast been exceeding good and gracious towards mee, which I humbly acknowledge, especially in vouchsafing so great and manifold blessings to me thy most unworthy servant in this thy present favour, which thou hast been pleased to make me partaker of amongst thy children. Now, deare Lord, make me ever truly thankfull with all my heart and soule unto thee for all thy mercies bestowed on mee, who with shame and sorrow doe confesse, I have deserved no good, but all evill at thy hands by my manifold offences committed against thee; therefore in all humility I doe beseech thee, to cast all my sinnes and wickednesse out of thy sight, and let them be no hindrance to thy grace and mercy towards me; but Lord still continue and increase thy

X   fatherly

fatherly care and loving kindnesse both to my
soule and body to prevent and preserve me from
falling into any sin or evill ; and vouchsafe to bestow all spirituall graces on mee, that may inable
me to live a more holy and acceptable life before
thee ever hereafter; and seale thou my pardon for
all my sinnes past, for Christ Jesus sake, who dyed
for me, and with his owne unvaluable bloud paid
my ransome, and fully satisfied thy great and just
wrath against me. But gracious God, how unspeakable is thy goodnesse and infinite favour towards mankinde, that instead of powring down
punishments upon us for our great offences a-
gainst thee, thou didst thy selfe in thy tender love
ordaine the meanes for our redemption, justification and eternall salvation ; through Christ thine
owne deare Son : praised be thy glorious Name
for ever, and chiefly at this time I magnifie thee
sweet Jesus (the mirrour of mercy) who before
thou hadst finished the great worke of our redemption, didst also institute the blessed Sacrament of
thy holy Supper that inestimable benefit, to all
thy servants which rightly receive the same, it
being a pledge of thy love, a remembrance of thy
mercy, a renuing of grace in us, a testimony of
thy favours, a confirmation of our faith, a uniting
of us (by thy Holy Ghost) to our blessed Lord and
head Christ Jesus, and all our fellow members in
perfect charity one towards another, with assurance thereby of the pardon of all our sinnes, and
                                        eternall

eternall salvation to our soules : the great benefit thereof is beyond my expression , of which this day thou haſt graciouſly vouchſafed to make mee (though unworthy of my ſelfe) yet by thy favour a happy partaker. Now deare Lord, enlarge thy goodneſſe further toward me thy poor ſervant, to give me daily the ſpirituall gifts of ſound repen-tance , encreaſe of true faith to beleeve all thy gracious promiſes , with grace rightly to apply them to my owne ſoule, and all the infinite bene-fits which thou my deare Saviour haſt purchaſed for me , that ſo this Sacrament may worke thoſe good effects in me which thou haſt therein offered unto us; and that I may by thy aſſiſtance , bring forth the fruits of righteouſneſſe, obedience, and true holineſſe of life, all the reſt of my daies, and to make ſuch thankfull and conſtant acknowledge-ment and right uſe of all thy mercies,as I may glo-rifie thy bleſſed Name ; reforme my waies , and frame my heart in all things to be faithfully and conſtantly thine, and then I know that thou wilt ever be my gracious God , to thy honour and my endleſſe felicity,through my Lord Jeſus Chriſt the righteous. Amen.

1. *A meditation concerning death.*

O Lord God Holy Ghoſt, our ſanctifier, pre-ſerver and comforter, who beſt knowes my corrupt nature , that cannot of my ſelfe performe

any

any true service towards God , being inclined to all evill, and unapt to any goodnesse, I humbly beseech thee, that understandest my manifold infirmities , be pleased to indue me with all saving graces in the performance of all holy duties towards God. And I humbly pray thee sweet Jesus to call and draw me daily unto thee ; and vouchsafe Lord by thy holy Spirit to possesse my heart and soule , to make mee wholly and constantly thine, truly to feare and love thee, to serve and obey thee in all things , that so thou in thy infinite mercy maiest never leave me, but be my gracious Lord , and mercifull God for ever.   And I humbly pray thee Lord Holy Ghost , to sanctifie and assist me thy poore sinfull servant, with all spirituall graces for my salvation in Christ , both living and dying , that I may strive to become what I ought to be, and to doe thy holy will in all things while I live. Now O good God, Father, Son, and Holy Ghost , thou knowest that many and evill have been my daies in this world, and by thy providence I have attained to a great age , but have not performed the ends for which I came into the world, who being made only to serve God in holinesse and righteousnesse all the daies of our lives to his glory, and our salvation, which is the chief thing needfull ; but alas, for the most part it is the least regarded or thought upon, where I confesse (with sorrow) that I have been too much neglectfull , having sometimes been drawne by the

cares

cares and troubles of this life , which neceſſity
brought upon me , to ſet my heart ever carefully
upon earthly things, and likewiſe, too often have
I been carried away with the vanity of my owne
heart in following after the preferments , or vanity of my owne ~~life~~, in following ~~after the pre-
ferments~~, or delighting in the pleaſures of this vile
world, all which periſh in the uſing, by which de-
luſions and deceits, that old ſubtill ſerpent Sathan
(that firſt wrought our ruine) he now ſteals away
our time and hearts, only to make us loſe our ſouls
alſo.   But deare Lord , though I have too long
gone aſtray , yet while I am going towards my
God, Lord let it be thy worke of grace and mercie to make me ſee and underſtand when I am out
of the right way before I goe too far to fall into
irrecoverable danger, from which I cannot returne. Oh ſhew me the paths of life and lead mee
into the true way to heaven that I may firſt turne
to thee in true faith with a contrite ſpirit , and a
broken heart for my loſt time paſt which I have
miſpent , that ſo I may obtaine pardon for all my
ſinnes formerly committed before thee , and then
I know thou wilt receive me as one of thine, and
in mercie bring me to thy ſalvation. Now Lord,
although our times are only knowne to thee, yet I
cannot have long to live, for the life of man is but
ſhort, and old age laden with infirmities and ſickneſſe is a ſure meſſenger and forerunner of death,
and then draweth near the firſt appearance when
K 3   my

my breath ceaseth, of my poore soule before the
tribunall seat, of thy great Majesty, O God, and
before all thy holy Angels there to bee called to
give an account of all my life and time mispent :
Alas, how can I answer one thing of a thousand;
now what should I doe, if I had not there in heaven an All-sufficient Saviour, who is also my
blessed advocate to mediate for me, in whom is all
my trust, comfort and confidence; therefore gracious Lord Jesus helpe me now while I am here,
and assist me to make my peace (as thou dost ad-
vise) while I am in the way before the grim and
cruell Sergeants of sicknesse and death lay hold
upon me to prevent me of the freedome, and ability of my senses, and spirit, being aided with thy
power, strength and grace by unfaigned repentance, and true faith to obtaine through Christ
my release, and pardon of those grievous debts
and trespasses that I stand guilty of before God,
which I am no waies able to satisfie, but only by
thee my Saviour Jesus, or else I shall be throwne
into that dreadfull dungeon, from whence there
is no escaping : Therefore now I doe most humbly beg and pray thee, that I may finde such favour in thy sight, knowing my owne disabilities,
that thou Lord wouldest frame and prepare my heart
and soule, for thine owne mercifull acceptance,
before thou call and cease upon me by death, to
take me out of this life, and make me continually
mindfull of my last end while I live, in health, and

of

of that ſtrict reckoning which then I muſt make
unto thee, the great God of heaven and earth, who
ſeeth and knoweth all things of all my life paſt, e-
ven to my very words. And let me ſtill remember
that thou Lord ſearcheſt the hearts and trieſt the
reines, and beholdeſt all our waies, and will
bring each worke to judgement, with every ſe-
cret thing, whether it be good or evill : Therefore I moſt humbly beſeech thee, while I am in
this world, give me the grace of daily and unfaigned repentance for all my ſinnes paſt, with
care to amend all my former faults in the reſt of
my life, and narrowly to examine my own heart,
ſoule and conſcience of all the evills I have done
before thee, hating and ſeverely judging and condemning my ſelfe for them, that ſo I may eſcape
thy great wrath, and not be judged and condemned by thee, O Lord, in thy heavy diſpleaſure,
which I am not able to beare ; for who can ſtand
in the ſight of thy great Majeſty when thou art
angry ? Therefore gracious God, let me here obtain thy mercifull pardon for all my offences paſt,
with grace to reforme my former miſdeeds, and
by thy bleſſed aſſiſtance become a new creature
all my daies, that ſo I may gaine a bleſſed end,
through my Saviour to dye in him, and make my
peace with God here, before I goe hence and be
no more : To which purpoſe I humbly pray thee
while I live, to make me a true and faithfull member of thy right Church & Kingdom of grace here

K 4   to

to professe and practice true Religion, and all holinesse of life to my last end ; but chiefly, Lord,
give me a blessed part in the first resurrection, that
I may not lye dead in trespasses and sinnes , but
may by thy holy Spirit be daily raised from the
grave of sinne, and enabled to live the life of
grace, that so the second death may have no power to hurt me; and at the last when it shall please
thee to appoint a stop to my daies, and to set a period unto my time, grant that my death be neither
suddaine, nor unexpected, neither my paines violent, whereby I should be unable, faithfully, earnestly and constantly to cry unto thee my God,
and call upon thy holy Name , for reliefe and
comfort in that great and dreadfull day and time
of death and danger , when my soules enemies
will seek my utter destruction; then Lord, depart
not from me , but pray that my faith in thee faile
not, and strengthen my weaknesse by thy power,
and supply my soule with all saving graces, and
defend me from the malice and subtill temptation
of my spirituall adversaries ; that they may never
be able to prevaile against me in any thing. But
I humbly pray thee sweet Saviour , to grant that
in the day of thy great visitation, my poore name
through thy unspeakable goodnesse, may be then
found written in thy blessed booke of life, so that
my sinnes, nor my soules enemies, may not be able
to blot it out , but that by thy infinite mercy and
favour, sweet Jesus, unto me , I may then be accounted

counted in thee worthy to escape thy just wrath, and by thy power and clemency, who didst vouchsafe to be borne of a woman, and shalt bee judge of the whole world, grant through thy mercies, merits, and manifold sufferings, that I poore sinfull creature, may be made able to stand before thee the blessed Son of God and man in that great and dreadfull day of judgement, when all our secret wickednesses shall be made manifest, and thou Lord, to whom all judgement is given by the Father, art to give our finall sentence : Oh then dear Jesus, in whom only I trust, receive me into thy gracious favour as one of thine, that my sinnes may be covered with thy righteousnesse, that so I may be preserved from thy wrath, and that wofull doom, Go ye cursed into hell fire, appointed for the Divell and his Angells; but Lord, in the fulnesse of thy mercy, make me one of that happy chosen number, to whom that joyfull call shall belong, Come ye blessed of my Father, inherit, and enter into that Kingdome, which he hath prepared for you before the beginning of the world ; and also thou our Saviour hast purchased for us ; then Lord in thy infinite love grant me a part in that everlasting happinesse, to live with thee , and glorifie thee there, for ever and ever. Amen.

2. *A*

2. *A Prayer to live blessedly, and dye happily.*

OH gracious Lord God, who didst create all things by thy omnipotent power, and lastly made mankinde I thou best knowest the frailties and corruption of our wretched nature which we inherit from our first parents, whose substance was but earth, and we are of our selves inclined onely to earthly and evill things, and such is the condition of mortall man, that all that are borne must dye, and returne to dust from whence they came, but the spirit returnes to thee, O God, that gave it, to receive either joy or blisse with thee for ever, or else eternall banishment from thee, who art the only good; therefore I doe most humbly beseech thee, deare Lord, to looke mercifully upon me, to helpe my manifold infirmities, and daily to prevent and keep me from falling into any sinne or evill to offend thee. But especially in the time of my death, dear Lord, be mercifull unto me a most miserable sinner, to forgive all my sinnes and offences past, that I have committed against thee my God, my brethren, or my owne soule; and grant through the merits, and many sufferings of thy beloved Son, and my only Saviour Jesus, that they may never bee imputed unto me thy poor servant, but vouchsafe good God, in thy manifold mercies to indue mee thy most unworthy suppliant, with all saving graces leading
to

to my salvation both in life and death;for we daily
see by example how suddainly death may surprise
us when we least expect it; therefore while this
life is in being, and I am going on in the way of
all flesh, which can be of no long continuance;
Lord teach and assist mee to make my peace for
my offences with thee my God while I am here,
who else wilt take an account of me in a dreadfull
place, and art able if thy wrath be not pacified,to
cast me into hell fire, from which there is no redemption; therefore have mercy on me,sweet Jesus, that I may by thy helpe, grace and assistance,
rightly fit and prepare my self for thy acceptance
before sicknesse lay hold on me ; for when death
seiseth it will carry mee immediately before the
judgement seat of thy great Majesty : Oh there let
me finde thee, deare Jesus, to be my gracious Saviour and Advocate, and so I shall obtaine mercy
and favour, and by thy sufferings, my offences
pardoned, and Gods severe justice satisfied. And
thus in thee and through thee only,my blessed Redeemer Iesus Christ, I shall be received to grace
and mercy,and made partaker of eternall life,and
remaine with Almighty God, in whose presence
is the fulnesse of joy, and at his right hand there
are pleasures for evermore, which Lord make me
partaker of, there to glorifie the Name of Almighty God, Father, Son, and Holy Ghost, for
ever. Amen.

3. *A*

3. *A Prayer to be prepared for a happy death,* *and to gaine a joyfull resurrection.*

MOst glorious Lord God, who didst make all things, thou well understandest that we poor creatures (how highly soever we are conceited of our selves) are but dust and ashes, and must returne to earth from whence we came ; our lives and times are in thy hand and power , and what thou hast appointed we cannot change , and all things to our selves are most uncertaine; for when thou with just rebuke dost chastise man for iniquity , thou makest his strength and beauty to consume away like a flower of the field that withereth and falleth : for when thou callest, man cannot retaine the spirit , nor adde one houre to his time, but it returnes to thee that gave it , and hee goeth downe to the grave , from which he shall not returne againe till this world is at an end : Therefore, deare Lord , I now most humbly beseech thee, for thy beloved sonnes sake, who hath satisfied thy just wrath by his infinite and innocent sufferings, and redeemed me from sin and Sathan by his death, Lord forgive and pardon me all my sinnes and offences past, either in soule or body, that I have committed against thee ever since I came into this miserable world, which I confesse are innumerable , more then the haires of my head, or the sand upon the Sea shoare, but vouch-

safe.

fafe, O mercifull God, to be reconciled unto mee
a wicked finner, in thy deare and righteous Son
Chrift Iefus my only Saviour, who hath paid my
ranfome with his owne pretious bloud, wherewith, oh God of mercie, blot my debt to thee by
finne, out of thy fight; and alfo he did fulfill all
righteoufneffe for me, who is now my bleffed Mediator in heaven, to impute all this unto mee:
Therefore, deare Lord Holy Ghoft, by thy gracious and holy Spirit, joyne and unite me unto my
Lord and head Chrift, never to be feparated from
him while I live here, and when I goe from
hence carry me to be where he is, and give mee
grace and faith in and through him, to make my
peace while I am in the way and paffage of this
life, and while I have breath to call upon thee,
before I am laid into the darke dungeon of the
earth, when the wormes fhall eat my corrupt
flefh; yet I truft and doe believe through him, that
hath overcome death, the grave, and hell for me,
t at at the bleffed refurrection of thy children and
fervants, that my corruption fhall put on incorruption, and I fhall fee my bleffed Lord and Saviour with thefe my eyes, who did redeeme me,
and fhall be my mercifull judge to fave me; therefore I have fure confidence in his favour, and under the wings of his mercie fhall I reft in fafety.
Now I humbly pray thee, O God the Holy Ghoft,
to fanctifie, fit, prepare, and affift my heart and
foule with thy Spirit, to fill me with all faving
graces

graces for my salvation; while I live, to enable
me to call, pray and strive to please thee here in
all things; but especially Lord at my death stand
by me and pray for me that my faith faile not: fit
and prepare me for thy gracious acceptance, before thou call and seise upon me to take me out of
this present life; and make me alwaies mindefull
both in health and sicknesse of my owne last end,
and then of my appearance before thee, to make
answer before the great God of Heaven & Earth
(from whom nothing can bee hid) of all my life
and deeds past, even to my very words; for thou
art only, and above all to be feared, who canst
both save and kill, and cast both soule and body
into utter perdition in hell: Therefore Lord,
vouchsafe to assist me with thy grace to worke in
me all things which may make me acceptable unto thee before the day of my departure, that when
it doth approach it may not bee fearfull and terrible, but happy and comfortable unto me in Christ
Jesus my Lord, that through him, my last day may
be my best, and most welcome to my soule; that I
may then call and pray, and say with confidence,
Come Lord Jesus, come quickly, for into thy hands
I most humbly commend my spirit, for thou hast
redeemed me, O Lord God of truth; and vouchsafe thou even to my last breath, alwaies to say
unto my soule, thou art my God, and my salvation
for ever. Amen.

x *yt f* may obtaine mercy x

4. *A Prayer in sicknesse, with expectation of death.*

OH heavenly Father, who haſt been my gracious God before I had being, and my mercifull guide from my youth, be pleaſed eſpecially now at the houre and point of my death which I ſhall ſhortly expect, to be mercifull, O God, unto me a miſerable ſinner, to pardon for Jeſus ſake all my ſinnes and iniquities that I have committed formerly; and vouchſafe to heale and ſave my wretched ſoule that hath infinitly offended thee, and ſtrengthen my weakneſſe with thy power, and ſupply all graces wanting in me by thy mercie, and defend me from all my ſpirituall adverſaries, who will endeavour my deſtruction if they can, but let them not prevaile againſt me; and Lord Jeſus, be not farre from me, neither forſake me in a time when ſo much trouble and danger is about me; but in the multitude of thy mercy, Lord pray for mee that my faith faile not, and ſtretch forth thy hand to ſave me, as thou didſt to *Peter*, leſt I periſh. Now, O God, give me ſuch ſound and unfaigned repentance, as may obtaine from thee remiſſion of all my ſinnes, with true faith to lay hold of all thy gracious promiſes, and a right and a ſtedfaſt hope in all thy mercies; but chiefly indue me with devout and perfect love toward thy Majeſty, which may make me faithfully and con-

constantly thine to serve and obey thy holy will
in all things, with Christian charity towards all
my brethren : but Lord; if it be thy will give mee
knowledge of my death when it is neare, that I
may faithfully pray unto thee, and call on thy
most blessed Name with my last breath, and may
joyfully and willingly yeeld up and commend my
spirit backe to thee my Lord, who gave it unto
me : And deare Lord, prevent and remove all e-
vill hindrances in my way to heavenly happinesse,
that through Christ Jesus my Saviour, I may bee
received amongst thy children and servants, and
admitted into the presence of thy Majesty, O
heavenly Father, there to enjoy eternall felicity
with thee in heaven when this life is ended by
death. But if thou shouldest please at this time to
continue and prolong my daies upon earth; Lord,
so long as I live, teach me by thy grace so to number my daies that I may apply my heart to wisdome and godlinesse and holinesse of life, seeking
to redeem my lost time past which I have mispent,
by daily repentance and amendment of life, striving to make my calling and election sure ; by a
holy and good conversation the rest of my time to
come, that by thy mercy, and merits of my Saviour Jesus I may be freed of my trespasses, and heavy account with thee before I dye, and may escape thy just and great wrath which is due for
my manifold transgressions.   Now Lord Jesus, I
willingly submit my selfe to thy good pleasure to
disjose

difpofe of me as thou feeft beft : but I moft humbly beg of thee, when my laft and appoin'ed hour
is come, that I fhall enter into my long fleep of
death, and goe to lye downe in the duft ; deard
Lord, give me a happy departure out of this life,
that I may dye in thee, O Lord, to reft in peace and
fafety, and may be raifed up by thee at the laft day
to grace and glory, that thou receiving mee into
thy mercy and favour, I may live and remain with
thee in eternall happineffe to glorifie thy bleffed
Name, and fing hallelujah amongft thy Saints for
ever and ever. Amen.

5. *A. Prayer unto the Lord of mercy in the time of
ficknesse to be fitted for death, and affisted in that
dreadfull houre againft all temptations, to gaine a
bleffed passage out of this world at Gods appointed
time.*

Great and mercifull God, who reigneft and
difpofeft of all things in heaven, and in the
whole world as it pleafeth thee, and underftandeft all the paffage here below on earth, be it never
fo fecret, and by thy mercie and power doft work
all things to the beft for thofe that love and depend upon thee; for thou art full of goodneffe, patience and long-fuffering towards us poore weak
and fraile creatures, and thy abounding mercy,
doth exceed all other thy great workes in pardoning finners; but beyond all other thy favours to-

L.   wards

wards us, thy infinite love to mankinde did most
appeare in sending thine owne dear Son into the
world to save sinners by thy grace, that all that
beleeve in him might be saved; without which thy
mercie, what hope, comfort, or helpe were there
left unto us miserable sinfull creatures; for the just
man falleth seven times a day, but the wicked
much more, and if the righteous scarcely be saved,
where shall the ungodly and sinner appear, such
as I am? Therefore I come and cry and pray unto
thee, who only canst relieve me, in all humility,
contrition and confession of my manifold transgressions, and in the blessed Name of thy dear beloved Son, my only Saviour, I do beg and beseech
thee, O Father, full of compassion, not to enter
into judgement with me, nor to remember what
I have done amisse; but to consider what thy Christ
hath done and suffered for mee, and looking on
mee through him, have mercy and pity upon me
a most grievous sinner; I know too well, how
justly thou maiest condemne me; but Lord, to save
a poore sinner by thy grace is farre greater honour and glory unto thee : And gracious God,
who of thine owne meer mercy didst give us thy
most deare Son to be our reconciliation and redemption whe wewere thine enemies, much more
being reconciled, and having performed all things
for us, thou canst deny us no good thing that wee
aske in his beloved Name : Therefore, O God,
for Christ innocent sake, vouchsafe to be reconciled

ciled unto me, thy moſt unworthy ſinfull ſervant,
and caſt all my offences into his grave, where my
Saviour paid the laſt part of my ranſome ; and by
his power riſing againe the third day from death,
he conquered and overcame all my ſoules enemies, ſin, death, hell and Sathan; and deare Lord,
with his pretious bloudſhed upon the croſſe, waſh
my ſoule cleane before it appeare in thy preſence,
and take away all my iniquities out of thy ſight,
never to ceme in remembrance before thee , ſo
that Chriſt may be unto me both in life and death
an advantage. And now moſt deare God, my life
and time here is only in thy hand and pleaſure, and
thou haſt caſt me upon the bed of ſickneſſe , from
which I know not whether I ſhall recover, or
riſe any more while I live in this world; therefore
I moſt humbly pray thee , ſweet Jeſus , never to
leave or forſake me, but ſtand thou alwaies in
mercy by me , and let thy right hand uphold and
ſuſtaine me to preſerve me from all my ſpirituall e-
nemies that wait to deſtroy my ſoule : But thou
my Lord, art ſufficient for me, O Lord, vouchſafe
me thy grace to direct my heart and words towards thee, and by thy ready helpe to aſſiſt me in
all things , and at all times, that in thy mercie at
the laſt thou maieſt finiſh all thy favour in mee,
which is the accompliſhment of my faith and
hope in thee: And Lord grant that I may willingly and readily come unto thee when thou calleſt;
and vouchſafe , O bleſſed Spirit Holy Ghoſt, to

L 2   fit

fit and prepare me by unfeigned repentance to obtaine remiſſion of all my ſinnes that I have done before thee, with true faith to lay hold of all the mercies of my God in Chriſt, and with ſtedfaſt hope to reſt on all thy gracious promiſes, O Lord, who never faileſt thoſe that truſt in thee.   Now Lord, give me ſtrength and patience to wait thy good leaſure and pleaſure, untill thou have pity and compaſſion on me, either to recover and reſtore my health here (if it be thy will) that I may live and glorifie thee longer in this life, or elſe that thou wilt pleaſe to receive and prepare me for thy ſelfe, and give me all ſaving graces for thine own mercifull acceptance, when thou pleaſeſt to call and take me to thee out of this wretched world, that ſo my faith and ſure truſt in thee may never faile unto my laſt breath. Now laſtly, Lord grant, that as the outward man (the body) decayeth and groweth weaker, ſo the inward part (the ſoule) may by thy gracious aſſiſtance grow together in faith and confidence towards thee, with full aſſurance of thy Spirit within me of thy favour to me for my eternall ſalvation : Then come Lord Ieſus when thou pleaſeſt, for into thy hands I humbly commend my ſpirit, that when this life ſhall leave me, thy grace and mercy may receive mee into that endleſſe happineſſe in heaven, which my Lord and only Saviour hath purchaſed for me, that I may praiſe God everlaſtingly. Amen.

6. *My*

6. *My Prayer of thanksgiving after my long and great fit of sicknesse, which began on Twelfth day at night and held me till Whitsontide : This may serve upon any other occasion.*

MOst gracious Lord God, I blesse and praise thy great and holy Name, for all thy blessings and benefits both spirituall and temporall vouchsafed to my soule and body; but especially I magnifie thy glorious Majesty for all those spirituall graces thou hast bestowed upon my soule before I was borne and hitherto, which I beseech thee of thy mercie daily to continue and increase towards me : Now deare Lord, make me thy unworthy servant ever truly thankfull to thee for all thy goodnesse extended towards me, and grant me grace to make such right use of all thy mercies as may be most to thy glory, and my salvation in Christ. But now, O Lord, that art my God, I must at this time render thee humble thanks in patticular, and not forget to acknowledge thy benefits, and to praise thy holy Name for all thy mercies shewed unto me; for in my late and long sicknes thou hast heard my groanes, and taken pity on me, and released me from all my paine and griefs, for thou dost visit my transgressions with favour (not in wrath) and hast alwaies been my stay and comfort from my youth, and thou art my deliverance and ready helpe in all my adversities, thou

L 3　　　　　didst

didst bring me downe for my sinnes almost to the
grave, and hast in mercy lifted me up again from
the gates of death, and restored me to health, who
healest all my infirmities, pardonest all my iniquities, and givest me present supply in all my necessities, blessed be thy glorious Name for ever. Now
O God, as thou art pleased to prolong my dayes
on earth, so especially I humbly pray thee daily
to increase all saving graces in mee for thy true
and faithfull service, and vouchsafe alwaies to
continue all thy goodnesse and mercies towards
me, that I may truly feare, perfectly love, and
carefully obey thee in all things; and by the assistance of thy holy Spirit, make me to become, and
ever to continue to bee more and more thy unfeigned servant : And now I am aged, and fit to
leave the world when thou pleasest, yet while I
am in it, Lord make me continually to grow from
grace to grace unto the knowledge of the Lord
Jesus Christ, with faith in him rightly to please
and praise thee so long as I live. And gracious
Lord vouchsafe never to withdraw thy grace and
favour from me, untill thou hast finished thy greatest worke of mercy, and the height of my hopes,
and happinesse, which is the salvation of my poor
soule, through thine owne deare Sonne, and my
only Saviour Jesus Christ; and when it shall please
thee to call me away to thy selfe out of this vaine
world, be pleased to give me a happy and blessed
departure to dye in my Lord Jesus, and in thy true
faith

faith and favour, that thou having pardoned all my
fins, and paſſing by my unworthineſſe, in Chriſt,
thou maieſt after death receive and accept mee
poore ſinner into thy grace and favour, through
thy dearly beloved Sonne, in whom only thou art
pleaſed, who is my righteouſneſſe, Lord, and my
Redeemer; and ſo when I have left this life, I ſhall
reſt in peace and ſafety, ſleep in Chriſt, and bee
raiſed by him hereafter to great glory amongſt his
ſervants, and may obtaine favour to be accepted
into the ſociety of holy Angels and bleſſed Saints,
and admitted into the glorious preſence of Almighty God, there to praiſe and magnifie his
Name, for ever and ever. Amen.

7. *My concluſion. A Prayer to my bleſſed Lord,*
and Saviour Jeſus Chriſt.

OH my deare Lord Jeſus, I moſt humbly begge
for thy love and mercies ſake to pardon all
my ſinnes paſt, that thou maieſt looke downe in
pity and compaſſion on me, to heare the prayer
of thy unworthy ſinfull ſervant, who doth earneſtly intreat thee, to vouchſafe me thy gracious
and continuall helpe, protection and direction, in
all my weake endeavours, wants and troubles,
that ſo all my deſires wayes and actions, being
begun, continued, and ended in thee, I may bee
able rightly and faithfully to ſerve and pleaſe thee
at all times, really to love and honour thee above

all things, truly and carefully to feare and obey thee according to thine owne will; confidently to relye upon thee, and willingly to submit to thy pleasure in all my crosses and calamities;and constantly to praise and magnifie thy most worthy and holy Name, for thy great and manifold blessings and benefits bestowed upon me of thy meer grace and mercy : O my blessed Lord and Saviour Jesus Christ, who art the author and finisher of my good, and finally of my eternall salvation, to thee be all praise, honour and glory, for ever and ever. Amen.

8. *Another short Prayer.*

O Lord my God, have pity upon me that am a most miserable sinner, and full of frailty, unapt and unable to doe any good, I earnestly desire rightly to serve thee, but without thy grace and help I cannot doe it, a fit subject for thy great mercy. Dear Iesus, pardon all my sinnes past,and give me grace henceforth to become a new creature in thee,daily to attend thy service constantly, and to performe all holy duties which I owe unto thee faithfully;and to shun and resist all sinfull neglects towards thee carefully;that so while I live, I may duly feare and obey thee rightly and truly to love and praise thee, here and for ever. Amen.

F I N I S.

My owne Prayer in Meeter, or to be sung as a Hymne.

1 IN mercy Lord heare my requests,
  for which to thee I call,
My griefes are great, my soul's opprest,
 thou canst me helpe in all.

2 A gift of God I doe require,
 which Lord me not deny;
Give me thy spirit of grace and prayer,
 with this still me supply.

3 In thee Lord I confide alone,
 turne not away thy face;
My hearts desire to thee is knowne,
 I sue to have thy grace.

4 My vaine heart cleanse and knit to thee,
 and for thy service frame me;
Thy constant Spirit in me let stay,
 my raigning sinnes to slay.

5 From neglectfull wandring thoughts keep me,
 in my devotions free,
They draw away from God my soule,
 and all my service spoile.

6 No earthly things let me imbrace,
 or on this world cast my mind,
Thy Kingdome, favour and thy grace,
 make me still seek and finde.

M

7 For

7 For of my selfe no strength I have,
  to doe thy blessed will,
Thy helpe O holy Ghost I crave,
  my duties to fulfill.
8 O God I will not let thee rest,
  unlesse thou heare my prayer,
Till me thy servant thou hast blest,
  in granting my desire.
9 To pardon my offences great,
  and from all sinne deliver,
Lord make me thine in soule and heart,
  thy faithfull servant ever.
10 From all the sins that I have done,
  Lord quit me by thy mercies true,
And free me from those iudgements great,
  which for my sinnes are due.
11 O Christ thy mercy and grace now beg I,
  which Lord unto me grant,
That I in thee may live and dye,
  in heaven to be a Saint.
12 Amen, so be it Lord say thou with me,
  that I these gifts may obtaine:
Then shall thy servant ever praise thee,
  whose goodnesse is my endlesse gaine.
13 All glory, thanks and praise be to thee,
  that sitst on heavens Throne,
Who shewest mercy unto me,
  when I to thee make moane.

Other

Other short Verses to the like purpose.

1 *Lord lead me in thy truth, and thy right way,*
   Be thou my God I thee most humbly pray.

2 *Teach me thy will, and all thy Lawes divine,*
   Which to fulfill Lord make me wholly thine.

3 *To serve, love, feare, obey, and praise thee ever,*
   who from my sinnes and hell wilt me deliver.

A Rule which I have gathered out of the Scriptures
to my owne use, for the governing and ordering both
of soule and body at all times, especially in the ser-
vice of God, to make us acceptable to his majesty,
and to bring all blessednesse and happinesse to our
selves.

First, especially endeavour to make thy heart
cleane, upright and faithfull, without doubting, which is the chiefe receptacle of most good,
or all evill. Secondly, have an innocent and gratefull minde, thankfully to acknowledge all Gods
mercies and benefits, and requite all humane
courtesies as farre as thou canst. Thirdly, let thy
prayers to the Almighty proceed from lippes unfeigned, free from falshood or guile. Fourthly,
lifting up pure hands with a penitent, fervent, and
devout soule toward God. Seventhly, set a watch
                                                    before

before thy mouth, to prevent thy tong from wicked cursing, slandering, lying, dissembling and swearing. Eighthly and lastly, be sure to keep a good and cleare conscience in all things, both before God and towards all the world; this will be thy ready and true witnesse, a continuall feast, and a continuall consolation to thy selfe in this life, and an assurance of eternall happines hereafter.

But *Salomon* the wisest amongst the sonnes of men gives one short rule, for our duties towards God, were we but able to performe it; saying, Let us heare the end of all, feare God and keep his Commandements, for this is the whole duty of man, for God will bring each work to judgement, what ever secret thing, whether it be good or evill.

FINIS.

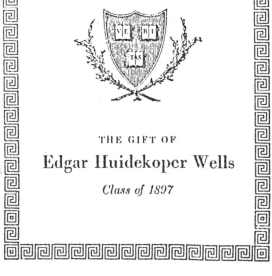

Susanna Bell, *The Legacy of a Dying Mother* (Wing B1801; B1802 in 1972 ed.) is reproduced by courtesy of the Trustees of the Boston Public Library. The text block measures 64 × 140 mm, page 46.

Page 54 is misnumbered as page 40.

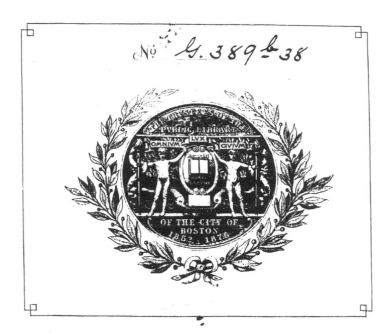

THE
LEGACY
OF A
DYING MOTHER
To Her
Mourning CHILDREN,
Being the
EXPERIENCES
OF
Mrs. *Susanna Bell*,
Who Died MARCH 13. 1672

With an
EPISTLE DEDICATORY
BY
THOMAS BROOKS Minister of the
Gospel.

LONDON,
Printed and are to be sold by *John Hancock*
Senior and *Junior* at the three Bibles in
Popes-Head Alley in *Cornhill*, 1673.

To his Honoured Friends,

Mr. T.B. I.B.. S.B. I T. Merchants, and to their Wives, and to the rest of the Children of Mrs. Susanna Bell deceased.; The Author wisheth all Grace, Mercy and Peace.

Honoured Friends,

MY Design in this Epistle is not to Complement you, but to benefit you; 'tis not to tickle your ears; but to better your hearts; nor 'tis not to blazon her name or fame to the World, whole Heaven-born-soul's now at rest with God, and who is swallowed up in those transcendent Enjoyments of that other World, which are above the comprehensions of my minde, and the Expressions and Praises of my Pen, but 'tis to a lure and draw you to a imitation of what was praise-worthy

A 2   in

in her.   Shall I hint at a few things.

First, imitate her in that sincerity and
plain-heartedness which was transparent
in her.   Sincerity is not a single grace,
but the Source of all graces, and the In-
terlineary that must run through every
grace, for what is faith if it be not unfein-
ed? and what is love if it be not without
dissimulation ? and what is Repentance if
it be not in truth ?   Sincerity is the soul
of all grace, 'tis the grace of all our graces; what advantage is it to have *the*
breast-Plate of Righteousness, the Shield
Eph. 6. *of Faith, the Helmet of Hope,* if they be
13, 14, but painted things ; it is the *Girdle of Sin-*
15, 16, 17 *cerity* that makes all the other parts of our
Armour useful ; Was she not a true *Na-*
Joh 1.4 *thaniel,* a Person in whom there was no
guile, I mean, no allowed hypocrisie :
and was not this that which carried her
through the pangs of death with a great
Isa. 38. 3, deal of comfort, as it had done *Hezekiah,*
2. *Paul,* and other Saints before.   A sincere
2 Cor. 1. Christian is like the Violet which grows
12. low, and hides it self and its own sweetness, as much as may be, with its own
leaves : Or like *Brutus* staffe, gold within and thorn without :   Or like the Ark
gold within, and Goats-hair without. The
very Heathen loved a candid and sincere
spirit

c A

spirit; as he that wished, *That there was a Glass-window in his breast, that all the World might see what was in his heart.* But

Secondly, imitate her in that Humility, which was a grace she was cloathed withal: I ever found her low and little in her own eyes; much in debasing her self upon all occasions, looking upon her self as below the least of mercies with *Jacob*, and *as dust and ashes*, with *Abraham*; and *as a poor worm*, with *David*; and *less then the least of all Saints*, with *Paul.* And commonly, the more high in spiritual worth, the more humble in heart; God delights to pour in grace into humble souls, as men pour in liquor into empty vessels. Humility makes a Person *Peaceable among Brethren, fruitful in well-doing, chearful in suffering, and constant in holy walking.* Humility makes a man precious in the eyes of God; who is little in his own account is always great in Gods esteem. It is well observed by some, That those brave creatures the Eagle and the Lion were not offered in sacrifice unto God; but the poor Lambs and Doves were,

1 *Pet.* 5.5

Gen. 32.
10.

Gen. 18.
27.

Ps. 22.6.
Eph. 3.8

A 3   10

to note, that God regards not your brave, high, lofty spirits; but poor, meek and contemptible spirits. Humility is a rare grace. Many (saith *Augustine*)can more easily give all they have to the poor, then themselves become poor in spirit; be low in your own eyes and be content to be low in the eyes of others; and think not of your selves above what is meet, as ever you would write after your Mothers Copy; and affect more to be amongst Gods little ones, then the great ones of this world. Be humble Christians; as ever you would be holy be humble; Humility is of the essence of the new creature: He is not a Christian that is not humble. The more grace the more humble; those that have been most high in spiritual worth, have always been most humble in heart. *Ignatius* could say of himself, *Non sum dignus dici minimus*, I am not worthy to be called the least. Lord, I am Hell, but thou art Heaven, said blessed *Hooper*; I am a most hypocritical wretch, not worthy that the earth should bare me, said holy *Bradford*. I have no other name, saith *Luther* then *Sinner*; *Sinner* is my name, Sinner is my sir-name: This is the name by which I shall be always known; I have sinned, I do sin, I shall sin *infinitum*.

Mat 18. 20.

Ruth

Ruth was the Daughter of the King of *Moab*, if we may give credit to the general opinion of the *Rabbines*, or if that be not so probable, yet she was one that we may well suppose to have been one of good quality in her own countrey, as being Wife of *Mahlon*, the elder brother of the Family of the Prince *Naasson*, yet she accounts her self scarce equal to one of the Maid-servants in the house of *Boaz.* So *Abigail* the wit of the time, 1 *Sam.* 25. 41. So *Elizabeth*, though she was the elder and the better woman for outward quality, yet how confounded was she with *Mary*'s visit, as being too great a weight of honour for her to bear. So *Mary*, *Luke* 1 38. If I were asked, said *Austin*, what is the readiest way to attain true happiness, I would answer, the first the second, the third thing is Humility. Humility doth not only entitle to happiness, but to the highest degree of happiness. *Mat.* 18. 4. Humility is that *Jacobs* Ladder which reaches from Earth to Heaven.

Ruth 2. 13.

Luke 1. 43.

Thirdly, imitate her in her charity and mercy towards suffering, needy, and wanting ones; how seldom did you find her ear or hand shut against charitable motions; she knew that those that did good to the

A 4   poor

poor and needy for Christs-sake, God would do good to them for the Poors sake, most sure for his Sons sake. She knew, that he who promised *They should have that asked,* had first commanded such to give unto them that asked; she knew that unmercifulness is a sin which least becomes, and worse beseems one that had so largely tasted of the mercies of God, as she had done both in New and Old *England.* She was much made up of pity and mercy to the poor, the bellies of the hungry, and the back of the naked, did often proclaim her pity and charity. Many Ministers, Widows and fatherless ones, have tasted, not only of her husbands bounty, but of hers also. Vain persons when they give, they will cause their kindness to run in a visible channel, they will sound a Trumpet to be seen of men; but was she not a secret and hidden Reliever of Gods distressed ones? Did she not refresh the bowels of many with her hid treasures? Will you all learn to write after this Copy? Of *Midas* it is Fabled, *That whatever he touched he turned into Gold;* 'tis most sure, That whatever the Hand of Charity toucheth, it turneth it into Gold. be

Mat. 6.
252.

it

it but a Cup of cold water, nay, in- *Mat.* 10. 42.
to Heaven it self; cold water ha-
ving not fuel to heat it, cold water
which costs not the charge of fire to
warm it. *Salvian* saith, that Christ
is *Mendicorum maximus*, the greatest
Beggar in the world, as one that
shareth in all his Saints necessities, *Heb.* 6.10
and will never forget the charitable
person, the merciful person. *Cicero*
could say, *That to be rich is not to
possess much but to use much*; And
Seneca could rebuke them that so stu-
died to increase their wealth, that they
forgot to use it. I have read of one
Evagrius a rich man, that lying upon his Death-bed, being importuned by
Synesius a pious Bishop, to give som-
thing to charitable uses, he yielded at
last to give three hundred Pounds,
but first took Bond of the Bishop that
it should be repayed him in another
world before he had been one day
dead. He is said to have appeared to
the Bishop, delivering in the Bond can-
celled, as thereby acknowledging what
was promised was made good, according to that promise, *Matth.* 19.
29 *And every one that hath forsaken
houses, &c.*

Fourthly,

Fourthly, imitate her in keeping off from the sins and pollutions of the day wherein you live; was she not one of Gods mourning ones for the abominations of the time? did not mens abomination in worship and practice vex, grieve, and wound her poor soul? was it not her great work to live by no Rule, to walk by no Rule, to worship God by no Rule, but by that which she dared to die by, and to stand by in the great day of our Lord Jesus? she knew, that worshipping of God in spirit and in truth was the great worship, the only worship that God stood upon. She did not, she durst not worship God according to the Customes of the World, or the Traditions of the Elders, or the Examples of great men; she knew that that Worship that is not according to the Word, is 1. Worshipping of devils and not God. Those that depart from the true Worship of God, and set upon false worship forbidden by God, do not serve God by it but the devil, what boasting soever they make, as you may evidently see, by comparing the Scriptures in the

Ezek. 9.4,6. *Jer.* 9.1,2. 2 *Pet.* 2.7, 8 *Psal.* 119.53. 136.158.

John 4. 23, 24. *Phil* 3.3, 2.

Rev. 9.20. 2 *Chron.* 11.15. *Amos* 5.25, 26. 1 *Cor.* 10.20. 1 *Tim.* 4.1. *Ezek.* 8.3.

the Margent together. She knew 2. That that worship that is not according to the Word is an Image of Idolatry, which of all sins is most provoking to a holy, jealous God. *The Devil*, saith *Synesius*, *is as glad to be worshipped in an Idol, as he was by* Israel *in a Calf*, there being nothing that provokes God to destroy poor sinners more then this. The learned Jews have a saying, *That no punishment ever happened to them in which there was not an ounce of the golden Calf*, grounding it on *Exod.* 32.34. *Nevertheless, I will remember to visit this sin upon them.* The *Egyptians* worshipped a pide Bull, and whereas some thought it strange, that when one died they should have another of the same colour. *Austin* thinks, that the devil, to keep them in idolatry, might do with their Cowes, as *Jacob* did with the Ewes, present to them when they conceived the likeness of such a Bull. Certainly Satan will use all the Art he can to keep poor sinners in ways of false worship, it being the most compendious way that can be to engage God to destroy them. She knew 3. That that worship that is not according to the Word, hath destroyed the most flourishing Churches and Nations, witness the Church and Nation

Exod. 32. 4.

Se. Hof.
5,5,6,7.
Rev. 9.
20. Ezek.
10.2.
2 Chron.
7.20.

Weems
Chrift.
Synag.

tion of the Jews, the feven Churches of *Afia*, and the whole Eaſtern parts of the Empire. She knew 4. That that worſhip that is not according to the Word is a curſed worſhip. It is the obſervation of one well ſkill'd in the Jewiſh Learning, that there is only one verſe in the Prophecy of the Prophet *Jeremy*, which is written in the *Chaldee* tongue, all the reſt being in *Hebrew*, and that is Jer. 10.11. *So ſhalt thou ſay, Curſed be the gods who made neither Heaven nor Earth;* and this ſo done by the Holy Ghoſt on purpoſe, that the Jews when they were in captivity, and ſolicited by the Chaldeans to worſhip falſe gods, might be able to anſwer them in their own language, *Curſed be your gods, we will not worſhip them, for they made neither Heaven nor Earth;* That God that made Heaven and Earth, is only to be worſhipped according to his own Word; for he will own no worſhip but what he will accept of, no worſhip but that; he will bleſs no worſhip but that, nor he will reward no worſhip but that; Your glorified Mother kept cloſe to inſtituted worſhip when ſhe had health and ſtrength; in this it will be your wiſdom to write after her fair Copy. But

Fifthly,

Fisthly, imitate her in justifying of the
Lord under the sharpest, bitterest, and
most afflictive Providences and Dispen-
sations; how often have I heard her to
justifie the Lord, even whilst he has been a   Joll 13.
writing bitter things against her; when   26.
Gall and Wormwood hath been put into
her Cup, hath she not said with *Ezra*,   Ezra 9.
God hath punished us less then our iniqui-   13.
ties deserve; and with *Nehemiah*, *How-*   Neh 9.
beit, thou art just in all that is brought up-   33.
on us, for thou hast done right, but we
have done wickedly; and with *Job, The*   Job 1.21
Lord gives, and the Lord takes, and bles-
sed be the Name of the Lord. And with
Daniel, The Lord our God is righteous   Dan.9.
in all his works which he doth. You know   14.
what afflictive Providences she has been
under, both in respect of her person,
and in the loss of her husband, and in
those variety of weaknesses that attended her body, and in the great
losses that some of you have met
with in this world: Besides several
other exercises; yet how has she
commonly been taken up in blessing
of God, and in justifying of God
and also in admiring the goodnesse of
God, that it has been no worse with her,
and

and here ; am satisfied she would not have exchanged her gains by afflictions for all the gains of this world. Stars shine brightest in the darkest night; Torches are better for the beating; Grapes come not to the proof till they come to the Press, Spices smell sweetest when pounded: Young Trees root the faster for shaking; Vines are the better for bleeding: Gold looks the brighter for scouring: Glow-wormes glitter best in the dark: Juniper smells sweetest in the fire: Pomander becomes most fragrant for chafing: The Palm-tree proves the better for pressing. Camomil, the more you tread it, the more you spread it : such is the condition of all Gods children, they are the most triumphant when most distressed; most glorious when most afflicted, as their conflicts so their conquests, as their tribulations so their triumphs. Gods people are true *Salamanders* that live best in the Furnace of afflictions; so that heavy afflictions are the best Benefactors to heavenly affections: when afflictions hang heaviest, then corruptions hangs loosest. And grace that is hid in Nature, as sweet-water in Rose-leaves, is then most fragrant when the fire of affliction is put under to distil it out. But

Sixthly,

Sixthly, imitate her in the standing, bent and course of her life and conversation. No man is to judge of the soundness or sincerity of his spirit by some particular acts, but by the constant frame and bent of his spirit, and by his general conversation in this world; if particular actions might determine whether a man had grace or no grace, whether he were in Christ or not in Christ, whether he were a *Saint* or no Saint, whether he were sincere or unsound, we should many times conclude, that those have no grace who indeed have, and that they were not in Christ who indeed are, and that they are no Saints who indeed are, and that they are not sincere, who certainly are true *Nathaniels*: the best Saints on this side Heaven have had their extravagant motions, and have very foully and sadly miscarried as to particular actions, (even then when the constant course and bent of their spirits, and main of their conversations have been Godwards, and Christ-wards, and Holiness-wards, and Heaven-wards, &c.) witness *Davids* Murther and Adultery, *Noah's* Drunkenness, *Lots* Incest, *Joseph's* swearing, *Jab's* cursing, *Jonah's* vexing, *Peter's* denying. and *Thoas* his not believing

Vna actio non denominat.

ing

ing; such twinklings do and will accompany the highest and fairest stars. As he that foots it best may be sometimes found all along, and the neatest person may sometimes slip into a slough. He that cannot endure to see a spot upon his clothes, may yet sometimes fall into a Quagmire. So the holiest and exactest Christians may sometimes be surprized with many infirmities and unevenneffes, and sad miscarriages. Certainly, particular sinnings are compatible with a gracious frame, though none are with a glorified condition. Our best estate on earth is mixt, and not absolute. Glory annihilates all sinful practices, but grace only weakens them. The most sincere Christian is but an imperfect Christian, and hath daily cause to mourn over his infirmities, as well as he has cause to bless God for his graces and mercies. Look as every particular stain doth not blemish the universal fineness of the Cloth. So neither doth this or that particular fact disprove and deny the general bent of a person's heart or life. Particulars may not decide the estate either way. 'Tis true, a man by a particular sinning is denominated guilty, but by no one particular can a mans estate be challenged either to be

good

good or bad. He that shall judge of a Christians estate, by particular acts, though very bad, will certainly condemn the Generation of the Righteous; we must always distinguish betwixt some single good actions, and a series of good actions; its not this or that particular good action, but a continued course of holy actions that denominates a person holy. Certainly, as there is no man so holy, but sometimes he falls into this or that particular sin; so there is no man so wicked, but he falls in with this or that particular duty: as you may (see in *Pharaoh, Balaam, Saul,* the *Ninevites, Felix, Herod, Judas,* yea, and the very Scribes and Pharisees. Now look as every sin which a godly man falls into (through infirmity) doth not presently denominate him ungodly; so neither will a few good actions done by a wicked man prove him godly: 'Tis what the course and tenour of the life is, that must be most diligently and wisely observed; for every man is as his course is; if his course be holy, the man is so; if his course be wicked, the man is so. There is a Maxim in Logick; viz. *That no general Rule can be established upon a particular instance;* and there is another Maxime in Logick, viz. *That no particular instance can overthrow*

B   *a*

a general Rule. We are never to make a judgement of our estates and conditions by some particular actions, whether they are good or evil; but we are still to make a judgement of our estates and conditions by the general frame, bent and disposition of our hearts, and by the constant tenour of our lives. Now I dare appeal to you and all others, that have observed the constant tenour of her life and conversation, whether it has not been such as becomes the Gospel, and as hath adorned the Doctrine of God our Saviour (humane infirmities excepted) And O that this might be the mercy of all her children, to walk with God as she hath done; and then I should not doubt but that they would all meet in Heaven at last. But

Seventhly, imitate her in her love to the Saints, to all the Saints, in whom she could discern *aliquid Christi,* any thing of Christ. Did she not love, delight and take pleasure to see the graces of the holy Spirit sparkling and shining in the hearts, lives and lips of the Saints, secretly wishing in her self that her soul were but in so noble a case. Were there any men in all the world, that were so precious, so lovely, so comely, so excellent, and so honourable in her account, in her eyes, as
those

Phil. 1. 27.

Tit. 2. 10

Gen. 6. 9.

1 John 3. 10, 14.

those that had the Image of God, of Christ, *Pf. 15. 1.*
of grace, of holiness, most clearly, 4.
most fairly, and most fully stampt *Pf. 16. 3.*
upon them. Did she not love Saints as *1 John 5. 1*
Saints ? Was it not the Image of God
that drew out her affection to the people
of God ? Many, like the *Bohemian* Curr,
can fawn upon a good suit; but grace
was lovely in her eye, though cloath'd
with Raggs. Many love godly men as
they are Politicians, or potent, or learned, or of a sweet nature, or affable, or
related, or as they have been kind to them;
but all this is but natural love; but to *1 Joh. 3. 9*
love them because they are spiritually *Pf. 45. 13*
lovely, because of the seed of God in
them, because they are all glorious within, is to love them as becometh Saints; it is
to love them at a higher and nobler rate
then any hypocrite in the world can reach
to. Did she not set the highest price,
and the greatest value and esteem upon
those that were gracious ? had she not an
honour in her heart for them that feared
the Lord ? Did she not value persons
according to their worth for another
world, and not according to their worldly
Greatness or Grandeur ? Did she not *Pro. 11.*
preferr a holy *Job* upon the dunghil, 26.
before *Pro. 28.*

before a wicked *Abab* upon the Throne? did she not set a higher price upon a gracious *Lazarus*, though cloathed with Rags and full of sores then upon a rich and wretched *Dives*, though he were cloathed gloriously, and fared sumptuously every day? was not her love to the Saints universal? to one Christian as well as another, to all as well as any, to poor *Lazarus* as well as to rich *Abraham*, to a despised *Job* as well as to an admired *David*, to an afflicted *Joseph* as well as to a raised *Jacob*, to a despised disciple as well as to an exalted Apostle? did she not love to see the Image and Picture of her heavenly Father though hung in never so poor a frame, and in never so mean a cottage; without peradventure, he that loves one Saint for the Image of God that is stampt upon him, he cannot but fall in love with every Saint that bears the lovely Image of the Father upon him. And O that this might be all your mercy to write after this Copy that she has set before you. But

Eighthly, imitate her in her constancy in the ways of God with a notwithstanding all the hazards, stormes, dangers and troubles that has attended those ways, especially in these latter days of Apostacy, wherein God had cast her lot. She was

not

Phil. 1.
21.
1 Pet. 2.
17.

not a Reed ſhaken with every wind; The
was unchangeable in changeable times,
whatever ſtormes beat upon the ways of
God, or the people of God, ſhe remain-
ed fixt, firm and immoveable in the ways *Pſal.* 44.
of the Lord; and doubtleſs ſuch ſouls as *Pſ* 119.
are truly good, they will be good in the 112.
worſt of times, and in the worſt of places;
and amongſt the worſt of perſons; Prin-
ciples of grace and holineſs, they are laſt- 1 *John* 3.
ing, yea, everlaſting; they are not like 9.
the Morning-cloud, nor the early dew. *Hoſ.*6.4.
Let times, and places, and perſons be what
they will, a ſincere Chriſtian will not diſ-
honour his God, nor change his Maſter,
nor quit his ways, nor blemiſh his Pro-
feſſion, nor wonnd his conſcience to ſleep
in a whole skin, or to preſerve his ſafety,
or to ſecure his liberty; and was it not
thus with her in the moſt trying times?
An upright man is a right man. שׁישׁ
Jaſhar is rendred by the Septuagint, *Judg.*
17.6. He is one that won't be bowed or *Gen.*6.9,
bent by the ſinful cuſtomes or examples of *Rev.* 14.
the times and places where he lives? Let 4. *Rev.*3.
the times be never ſo dangerous, licen- 4. *Job* 17.
tious, ſuperſtitious, idolatrous and erro- 9.
neous, yet a ſincere plain-hearted Chriſtian will keep his ground, and hold on
in his way, as might be made evident by

a

Heb: 12.
1.
Pf 125.
1,2.

a cloud of witnesses. The Lawrel keeps its freshness and greenness in the Winter-season; a sincere Christian is *semper idem*; let the wind, and the world, and the times turn which way they will, a sincere soul for the main will still be the same. He will be like Mount *Sion* which cannot be removed; he will stand his ground and hold his own under all changes; he is like the Philosophers good man (*Tetra-gonos*) four-square, cast him where you will, like a Dye he falls always square and sure; so cast a plain-hearted Christian where you will, into what company you will, and into what condition you will, yet still he will fall sure and square for God and godliness; let the times be never so sad, nor never so bad, yet a plain-hearted Christian will still keep close to God and his ways, and will rather let all go then let his God go, or his Religion go, or his Integrity go, or Ordinances go. *Lapidaries tell us of the Chelydonian stone, that it will retain its virtue and lustre no longer then it is enclosed in Gold;* a fit Emblem of an unsound heart, who is only good while he is enclosed in golden prosperity, safety and felicity. An unsound Christian, like green Timber, shrinks when the Sun of Persecution

shines

shines hot upon him; the heat of fiery trials cools the courage of unsound Christians; but a sincere plain-hearted Christian is like a massie-vessel of Gold, that keeps its own shape and figure at all times, in all places, and in all companies: when one of the Ancient Martyrs was greatly threatned by his Persecutors, he replied, *There is nothing (saith he) of things visible, nothing of things invisible, that I fear; I will stand to my Profession of the Name of Christ, and contend earnestly for the faith once delivered to the Saints, come on't what will, in these evil days wherein multitudes have turned aside into crooked paths.* She kept close and constant to the ways of the Lord, so long as her natural strength lasted. And O that all you her children would make it your business in this as well as in other things to write after your Mothers Copy; remembring, that if you are not faithful unto death, you shall never receive a Crown of life; *Rev.* 2. 10. And that if you do not continue to the end (that is, in well-doing) you shall never be saved, *Matth.* 24. 13. But

Ninthly, Imitate her in her high valuations of Jesus Christ, what low and little

B 4 the things

Phil. 3. 8, 9, 10.
Mat. 13. 44.

things were her own graces, duties, services and mercies, when she cast her eye upon Christ, when she fell into discourses of Christ. Christ was her (*Summum bonum*) chiefest good. What was all the world to a sight of Christ, to a day, yea, to an houres communion with Christ. They are no believers that don't value

1 Pet. 2. 7

Jesus Christ above all the world, and all things in the world; *for unto every one that believes he is precious*; most precious, only precious, and for ever precious. They value him 1 Above their lusts, *Gal. 5. 24.* They can pluck out right eyes for Christ, and cut off right hands for Christ. 2. They value him above the world. Witness *David, Psal. 73. 25.* and *Daniel, Dan. 6.* and the disciples, *Matth. 19. 27.* and *Moses, Heb. 11. 25, 26.* and the primitive Christians and the Martyrs of a later date. 3. They value him above their lives, *Rev. 12. 11. They loved not their lives unto the death.* So *Paul, Acts 20. 22, 23, 24. Acts 21. 13.* So the Martyrs. 4. They value him above all their Relations. If all the World were a lump of Gold (said the *Dutch Martyr*) and in my hands to dispose of, I would give it to live all my days with my Wife and Children in a Prison, but Christ and

his

his Truth is dearer to me then all. You
have thousands of such instances upon record. 5. They value him above their
goods, *Heb.* 10 34 *Ye took joyfully the
spoiling of your Goods.* So has many
thousands since under sharp persecutions.
6 They value him above all natural, spiritual and acquired excellencie , *Phil.* 3.
7, 8. in all my serious Discourses with her
about our Lord Jesus Christ, she would
still set the Crown upon Christs head. She
would lay her self low, very low, that
he alone might be exalted. The thoughts
of Christ was precious to her, the Discourses of Christ were precious to her, the
Image of Christ was precious to her, the
Ordinances of Christ were precious to her,
the Discoveries of Christ were precious to
her, the day of Christ was precious to
her, the Offices of Christ were precious
to her, and the Rebukes of Christ (whilst
she enjoyed his Presence under them) was
precious to her ; but above all, the Person of Christ was most precious to her ;
In her eye *he was the chiefest of ten thou*   *Cant.* 5.
sand, fairer then the children of men, and 10 *Psal.*
all the riches, honours, pleasures and de-   45. 1.
lights of this world were but dung in com- *Phil.* 3. 7,
parison of him. , O at what a rate has the 8.
Saints of old prized our Lord Iesus.
                                    Maliem

Mallem (said one) *ruere cum Christe, quam regnare cum Cæsare, Luther* had rather fall with Christ then stand with *Cæsar.* The same Author elsewhere saith; that he had rather be (*Christianus Rusticus* then *Ethnicus Alexander,*) a Christian-Clown then a Pagan-Emperour. *Theodosius* the Emperour preferred the Title of *Membrum Ecclesia* before that of *Caput Imperii*; professing that he had rather be a Saint and no King, then a King and no Saint. And godly *Constantine* rejoyced more in being the servant of Christ, then in being the Emperour of the World. *Bernard* saith, *That he had rather be in his Chimney-Corner with Christ, then in Heaven without him.* It was an excellent Answer of one of the Martyrs when he was offered riches and honours if he would recant, said, *Do but offer me somewhat that is better then my Lord Jesus Christ, and you shall see what I will say to you.* It was a sweet Prayer of one, *Make thy Son dear, very dear, exceeding dear, only dear and precious, or not at all.* Another good man cried out, *I had rather have one Christ then a thousand worlds.* I have read of *Johannes Mollius, That whensoever he spake of the Name of Jesus, his eyes dropt tears:* And of another Reverend
rend

rend Divine, who being in a deep muse
after some discourse that passed of dear
Jesus, and tears trickling down his cheeks
before he was aware, and being asked the
reason of it, he confessed ingenuously, *It
was because he could not draw his dull
heart to prize Jesus Christ at that rate he
should and fain would* Christ lay near
your Mothers heart, and O that he may
lie near all your hearts, that so you may
be safe and saved for ever But

  Tenthly, Imitate her in the casting a
Mantle of love over the infirmities and
weaknesses of poor, weak, miscarrying
Christians, in the burying of Christians
weaknesses under their graces ; much I
know of this, but some know much more.
She was not for blazoning of others weaknesses, whether they were nearer to her, or
more remote from her.   She commonly
carried a Mantle of love about her to cast
over other mens sins ; she seemed to live
under the Power of that Word, *Pro.* 10.
12. *Love covereth all sins* ; and that 1 *Pet,*
9.8. *Charity shall cover the multitude of sins.* By covering must be
meant, 1. A favourable Construction
of all things, which in right reason
might well be construed. 2. A passing
by smaller infirmities and private offences.
                                          3. Such

3. Such a covering as might cure alfo, for love is wife. Love hath a large Mantle, and covers all fins, that is all private fins, and all fuch fins as may be concealed with a good confcience, both towards God and towards men. Again, it muft be under-ftood, not of our own tranfgreffions committed againft God, but of other mens fins and tranfgreffions committed a-gainft us Love is not fufpicious but in-terprets all things in the beft fenfe. Love will not publifh private in-juries to the difhonour or fhame of the party offend-ing *Prov.* 12.16. A *prudent man covereth fhame.* It is recorded to *Vefpafians* honour, *That he was more ready to conceal the vices then the vertues of his friends.* Such commonly are beft acquainted with other mens infirmities, who are leaft ob-fervant of their own iniquities and irregu-larities. The nature of man is very apt, faith *Seneca,* (*Vtimur perfpicillis magis quam fpeculis*) to ufe Spectacles to behold other mens faults, rather then Looking-Glaffes to behold their own. *Erafmus* fpeaks of one who collected all the lame and defective verfes in *Homers* Works, but

Pro. 17.9

To obferve and take notice of other mens faults, but not of our own, is the eafieft thing in the World, faid Tha-les.

but-passed over all that was excellent. The *Donatists* of old were more glad to finde a fault then to see it amended; and to proclaim it then to cover it; to carp at it then to cure it. *If I should finde a Bishop committing adultery* (saith *Constantine* the Great) *I would cover that foul Fact with mine Imperial Robe, rather then it should come abroad to the scandal of the weak, and the scorn of the wicked.* Seneca unmasking the face of their corrupt State, hath this notable passage, *The News from Rome take thus, the Walls are ruined, the Temples are not visited, the Priests are fled, the Treasuries rob'd, old men are dead, young men are mad, Vices are Lords over all: The Dictator blames the Consul, the Consul checks the Censor, the Censor chides the Prætor, the Prætor falls foul upon the Ædile, and he casts all the fault upon the Quæstor, and because no man will acknowledge himself in fault we have no hopes of better times,* How applicable this is to our present times I shall leave others to judge; but by the whole you see that all sorts and ranks of men are more apt to observe and quarrel at other mens faults, then with their own Observable is that of our blessed Saviour, *Luke* 7. 37. *There was a woman in the*

City

City which was a sinner: No wonder,
what woman is not? we may guess both
who the woman was, and what the sin
was, and which City it was : but he neither names the City, nor the sin, nor the
sinner. Seeing her Reformation, he con-
sults her Reputation. O that you would
all labour to write after this Copy; When
Alexander was painted, the Painter laid
his finger on his wart, and *Apelles* covered *Venus* mole with her finger, that it
might not be spied. As you stand in a
near relation one to another, so I could
wish that you would lay your fingers
upon one anothers warts and moles, and
not blazon one anothers humane frailties
and infirmities to the world, but love,
and live as brethren and sisters, who are
never without a mantle of love to cover
infirmities, I say, not enormities : to cover weaknesses I say, not wickedness : to
cover from the world, I say, not from
God, nor from one another. But .

Eleventhly, Imitate her in her earnest
desires and endeavors, that others, especially that her nearest and dearest Relations might taste that the Lord is gracious, that they might all be holy and happy, gracious and glorious, that they
might all have changed hearts, renewed
                                    natures,

natures, and sanctified souls: That they
might all be born again, adorned with
grace, filled with the spirit, and fitted for Heaven. You know, that upon her dying bed, she desired me,
that when she was asleep in Jesus,
that I would, for the advantage of the
living, especially for your sakes (who
lay nearest her heart) preach on that
Psal. 34. 8. *O taste
and see that the Lord
is good.* Which ac-
cordingly I did, once
and again. Now what
was her design in this,
but that every one of
you might share with
her in the same favour,
love, spirit, grace, me-
rit, righteousness and

*1 Thes.4.14.
The three Sermons that I
preached on* Psal.34.8. *I
have been desired to Print,
but could not answer
Friends expectations in
that, because I had not the
Notes by me, of what I
said upon that Text.*

goodness, that her soul had long tasted of. There is not a soul that ever
have had any saving taste of the Lord, and
of his goodness, but is mighty desirous that
others should taste of the same grace and
goodness. *O taste and see that the Lord
is good.* : As if *David* should have said,
I for my part have seen, tasted, and experienced much of God and his goodness, and
never more then in my greatest streights.

I

I am loth to eat these heavenly viands, and soul-ravishing morsels of contentment alone   Come hither all you that fear God, and I will tell you what God hath done for my soul. Come, O come poor souls, taste and see with me how good the Lord is; how comfortable the embraces of Christ are; and how sweet communion with Heaven' is.   We cannot advantage others, more then by declaring and communicating unto them our soul-secrets, our soul-Experiments.   All the Saints own it as their duty to glorifie God in their Generation, and wherein can they bring more glory to God then in helping souls to Heaven? and how can they finde out a readier way to effect this great business, then by telling them what God has done for their souls; then by making a faithful Narrative of their own conditions, by nature and by grace; when and how the goodness of the Lord was made known unto them upon a saving account. O tell poor wounded sinners what methods of mercy the Lord used to the

heal-

Psf.66.16. the words are without a Copulative in the Hebrew, venite, audite. Calv. Come, Heaven. Like that Gen. 19.14. It not only imports an Invitation, but the affection also of him that speaks.

healing up of your wounds, and to the
quieting of your consciences; that so they
may be encouraged to a serious use of all
Gospel-means, and to a hope of the same
grace and goodness of the Lord towards
them. O labour more and more to con- *Heb.* 12.
vince others by your experiences, that 14.
grace is the only way to glory; and that *See my*
without holinesse no man shall see the Lord; *Treatise*
Paul had tasted that the Lord was good, *on this*
and he wish'd; that both *Agrippa* and all *Text.*
that heard him were altogether such as he *Acts* 26.
was, except his bonds. As soon as *Mat-* 29.
thew had tasted that the Lord was good; *Luke* 5.
he called together an huge multitude of 29.
Publicans and others to meet at his house.
As soon as *Philip* had tasted of the sweet-
nesse of communion with Christ, he runs *John* 1.
to *Nathaniel* to invite him to Christ, say- 45,46.
ing, *Come and see*. No sooner had the
Woman of *Samaria* tasted of Christs living waters, but she leaves her water-pot, *John* 4.
and posts into the City to call out her 28.
friends and neighbours to see and taste
how good dear Jesus was. So those
young Converts, *Zech.* 8.21. *And the*
inhabitants of one City shall go to another, Vide
saying, Let us go speedily to pray before the Pemble
Lord, and to seek the Lord of Hosts I'm *loc.*
will go also. Mic. 4.2. *And many Na-* Ha. 2.2,
tions 3,4.

tions shall come and say, *Come and let us go
up to the Mountain of the Lord, and to
the House of the God of Jacob, and he
will teach us of his ways, and we will walk
in his paths, for the Law shall go forth
of Zion, and the Word of the Lord from*
Hierusalem. These blessed Converts
would not come alone, but draw others
along in company with them to worship
the Lord, which is lively expressed in a
Mimesis or imitation of the encourage-
ments and invitations they should use
one to another, *I will go also :* every one
was as forward for himself, as zealous
for another. O blessed frame of spirit !
O my friends, it is the nature of true grace
to be diffusive and communicative ; Grace
can't be conceal'd; they that have tasted of
divine sweetness cannot chuse but speak of
it to others, their hearts like bottles of
new wine, would be ready to burst if they
had not vent. Grace is like fire in the
bones, they that have it cannot hide it.
All the faculties of the soul, and all the
members of the body, will still be a telling of others, that there is a treasure of
grace in the soul. The blind men that
were cured were charged to be silent, but
they could not hold their peace. So here,
Litmer becaumed, we therefore learn that

we

we may teach, is a Proverb among the Rabbins. And I do therefore lay in and lay up (ſaith the Heathen) that I may draw forth again, and lay out for the good of many. And ſhall not grace do as much as nature, ſhall not grace do more then nature? Well friends, this I ſhall only ſay, that the frequent counſels that your glorified Mother have given you to taſte of divine goodneſs, and the experiences that ſhe has communicated to you of her taſte of divine goodneſs, both in her health and ſickneſs, both in her living and dying, will certainly either be for you, or elſe be a dreadful witneſs againſt you, in the great day of our Lord Jeſus. O remember not only theſe experiences of hers, that are now preſented to your eyes; but thoſe other experiences of hers as to her inward man that has often ſounded in your ears, But

Laſtly, labour to imitate her in her comfortable paſſage out of this world. Thoſe words were more worth then a world which ſhe uttered a little before ſhe fell aſleep in the Lord, *viz. Lord, take my aking head, and lay it in thy boſome.* How often did ſhe expreſs her longings to be with Chriſt, that ſhe might ſir nor ſorrow to more her outward man was full of pain,

weak-

weakness and trouble, yet how was her inward man refresh'd and quieted in a way of believing, according to that blessed Word, *Isa.*26.3 *Thou wilt keep him in perfect Peace.* The Hebrew runs שלום שלום *Shalom, Shalom, Peace, Peace : whose mind is stayed on thee : because he trusteth in thee.*

In all my visits of her, my hardest task was still to work her into a willingness to stay in this world, till all her doing and her suffering work was over.

Never did the espoused Maid long more for the Marriage-day, nor the Apprentice for his freedom, nor the Captive for his Ransom, nor the condemned man for his Pardon, nor the Traveller for his Inne, nor the Marriner for his Haven, nor the sick man for his health, nor the wounded man for his cure, nor the hungry man for his bread, nor the naked for clothes, then she did long to die and to be with Christ. which for her was best of all.

Phil. 1. 23.

How often were those words in her mouth. *Come, Lord Jesus, come quickly.* The face of none is so comely to the Saints eye, the voice of none so lovely to his ears, the taste of none so pleasant in his mouth as Jesus Christ. The Name of Jesus hath a thousand treasures of joy and comfort in it, saith *Chrysostome,* and

Rev. 22. 20.

53

is therefore used by *Paul* five hundred times, as some have reckoned. The Name of a Saviour (saith one) *is Honey in the Mouth, Musick in the Ear, and a Jubilee in the heart:*. And how often was that blessed word in her mouth, *Remember, O Lord I beseech thee, how I have walked before thee in truth, and with a perfect heart, and have done that which is good in thy sight*; a serious sense of her uprightness in the main of her walking with God, did yield her more then a little sweetness and comfort when she was upon her bed of Pain; one of the last speeches of a dying upright Christian was this, *Satan may as well pluck God out of Heaven, as pluck my soul out of his keeping.* She knew him in whom she had believed, and was perswaded that he was able to keep that which she had committed to him a-gainst that day. A child that hath any precious Jewel given him, cannot better secure it, then by putting it into his fathers hands to keep; so neither can we better provide for our souls safety then by committing them to God : *Keep that which I have committed :* that is, either my precious soul, which I have committed to his care and custody to bring it forth glorious at that day of his appearance;

Bernard

*Isa.*38.3

John 10. 28, 29, 30. 2*Tim.* 2. 12.

C 3

or my eternal life, happiness and crown of glory, which I have as it were deposited with him by faith and hope; and thus it was with her. The Apostle saith, he committed to Gods Custody a Pawn or Pledge, but about this Pawn or Pledge Interpreters differ; One saith *It is his soul*; Another saith, *It is himself*; And a third saith, *It is his works:* And a fourth saith, *It is his sufferings*: And a fifth saith, *It is his salvation*. In short, he committed to God his soul, himself, his doings, his sufferings, to be rewarded with life and salvation; and so did she who is now at rest in the Lord. Lord (saith *Austin*) I will die that I may enjoy thee. I will not live, but I will die; I desire to die that I may see Christ, and refuse to live that I may live with Christ. The broken Rings, Contracts and Espousals, contents not the true Lover, but he longs for the Marriage-day, and so did she, who has now exchang'd a sick bed for a Royal Throne, and the company of poor Mortals, for the Presence of God, Christ, Angels, and the spirits of just men made perfect. It was well said of one, *So far as we tremble at death, so far we want love*; its sad when the Contract is made between Christ and a Christian;

stian ; to see a Christian afraid of the
making up of the Marriage : But your
deceased Relation was no such Christian ;
I know nothing in this world that her
heart was so much set upon, as the com-
pleating of the Marriage between Christ
and her soul. My eye is upon that text,
*Isa. 57. 1. The righteous perisheth, and
no man layeth it to heart, and merciful
men are taken away, none considering that
the righteous are taken away from the evil
to come.* I have read of one *Philo* a
Jew, and of another, that when they came
to any City or Town, and heard of the
death of any godly man, though never so
poor, they would both of them mourn
exceedingly, because of the great loss that
place had by the death of that godly man,
and because it was a warning Piece from
God of evil approaching ; but ah, how
many famous godly Ministers, and how
many choice Christians hath the Lord of
Hosts taken away from us, and yet who
lays it to heart. There is no greater
Prognostick of an approaching Storm,
then Gods calling home so many Wor-
thies (of whom this world was not worthy)
as he has lately done. Now O that God
would beautifie all your souls with all these
22 Jewels, with which your Mother was
adorned in life and death. Sir,

Sir, you having signified to me, that it was your Mothers minde, and your desires, that her following Experiences should be printed. I did think it might be somewhat seasonable to put you all in minde of such things as I had (among many others) observed, and which should be all your ambition to imitate, as you would give up your accounts at last with joy, and be happy with her for ever in that other world,

Considering, that these Experiences may fall into other hands besides your own. I thought it meet to let such Readers know, that these were taken from her by one of you; when she was in a very weakly condition, and had little more strength then to speak; and they are but some of those that lay most warm upon her heart at that time. God began to work upon her in the Morning of her days; and had there been a Collection of all her most close, inward, spiritual Experiences, they would have been greatly multiplied beyond what is now presented to the Readers eye; but that was a Task too hard for her under those variety of weaknesses that she was every day contending with. The Experiences of old disciples commonly rise high, but

the

the Ingenious Reader may easily discern
by the twelve Jewels with which she was
adorned, that she was a woman both of
choice and great Experiences, *Austin* ob-
serves on *Psal.* 16. 2. ‸ *Come and hear
all ye that fear God, and I will declare
what he hath done for my soul :* ‘ He
‘ doth not call them (saith he), to acquaint
‘ them with speculations, how wide the
‘ Earth is, and how far the Heavens are
‘ stretch'd out, or what the number of the
‘ stars are, or what is the course of the
‘ Sun ; But come and I will tell you the
‘ wonders of his grace, the faithfulness of
‘ his promises, and the riches of his mer-
‘ cy to my soul. Now all Ministers and
Christians that had any inward acquaint-
ance with her soul-concernments, they do
very well know, that she was most taken
up with the wonders of Gods free, rich,
and sovereign grace, and with the sweetness, the fulness, the freeness, the riches
and the faithfulness of his Promises, and
with the riches of his mercy in Christ to
her soul.

To draw to a close, it is observable,
that even the holy Apostles in their Ca-
nonical Epistles, have spent some good
part of their holy lines in the ample Commendations of those eminent Saints to
whom

to whom they wrote, as *Paul* in his
to *Philemon*, and *John* in that of his
to an Honourable Lady: and that
other to a meaner person, *viz. Gaius*;
and that they went not behind the
door (as we say) to whisper; but as
on the House-top did proclaim the
Religious and pious practices of those
more choice Christians to the imitation of others. And further, when I
consider that which the Apostle speak-
eth of, *Demetrius* a rare and not
ordinary Testimony; *Demetrius hath*
3 Ep. of *a good report of all men, and of the*
John 12. *Truth it self; and we also bear Re-*
cord, and we know that our Record is
true : And yet further, when I consider what is Recorded of *Hezekiah,*
Thus did Hezekiah throughout all Ju-
2 Chro. *dah, and wrought what was good, and*
31.20, *right, and true before his God.* And
21. in every work that he began, in the
service of the House of God, and
in the Law and Commandments, he
did it with all his heart and prof-
pered, And when I consider what
high commendations the Apostle be-
stows upon the Churches of *Mace-*
donia, 2 *Cor.* 8. 1. to. the eleventh
verse,

verse; And upon the Church of *Thes-
salonia,* 1 *Thessal.* 1. 1, 2, 3, 4, 5,
6, 7, 8, 9. And also 2 *Thessal.* 1.
3, 4, 5. And when I consider, that
it was the Holy Ghost who writ 2 *Chron.*
Jehoiada's Epitaph, *They buried him* 24.16.
in the City of David among the Kings,
because he had done good in Israel,
both towards God and towards his
house. It is said also of *Josiah,* in
his Commendations by the same Spi-
rit, *Like unto him there was no King,* 2 *King.*
Moses and *Miriam,* *Sarah,* *Debo-* 23.25.
rah, *Esther,* *Elizabeth* and others,
after their deaths have had their due
praises. When I consider of these
things I am very well satisfied in
what I have said concerning this deceased Sister and friend. I do no
ways doubt, but that we may very
safely say good of such, when dead,
whose ordinary course and practice it
was to do good while they lived;
but in this censorious Age, no sooner is dust cast upon some Christians heads, but there are those that
will do what they can to throw dirt
in their faces: *Augustine* doth very
fitly compare these to *Dives* his dogs.
                                        they

they lay licking and sucking Lazarus his
sores, but his sounder parts they never
medled with. To trample upon the Reputation, and stain the glory of them that die
in the Lord, argues such Persons to be a
kin to Fleas, who bite most when men are
asleep. It was one of *Solons* Laws, *that
none should dare to speak evil of the dead.*
And *Plutarch* tells us, *that that was highly commended and duly observed:* But is
it so now? This I am sure, that it well
becomes Christians not to dare to speak
evil (if they could) of those who for the
main have lived holily, and died graciously, as this deceased friend hath done.
Let this satisfie us, that she is above the
Praises and envies of men. 'Tis the
good, the profit, the advantage of all
your souls, and theirs into whose hands
this little Piece may fall, that has drawn
me out to write so large an Epistle. If
I had had only the dead in my eye, a few
lines should have serv'd the turn. I doubt
not but that you will kindly accept of my
endeavours to be serviceable to your im-
mortal souls, and who can tell what fruit
may grow upon this Tree? I shall im-
prove all the interest I have in Heaven,
that both the Epistle and your glorified Mothers Experiences may be blest, to
                                        the

the furtherance of the internal and eternal welfare of all your souls.   The goodwill of him that dwelt in the Bush, rest upon you and yours.   So I Rest

Honoured friends,

Your Souls Servant.

THO. BROOKS.

A
TRUE RELATION
OF

Some of the EXPERIENCES *of*
Mrs. SUSANNA BELL, *taken from*
her own Mouth by a near Relation of hers,
a little before her death.

Left as a LEGACY *to her Mourning*
Children.

IT pleased the Lord to order it so, that
in my young days I was cast into a Family that feared the Lord. And going to hear Mr. *White*, preaching from
those words, *Prov. 15. 15. But he that is of
a merry heart hath a continual Feast.* From
these words he did shew, how happy a
thing a good conscience was, and what a
sad thing it was with *Judas* to have a bad
conscience; and what a blessed thing it
was to have a good conscience. From that
of

of *Hezekiah,* *Isa.* 38. 3. And he said. Remember now, O Lord, I beseech thee, hou I have walked before thee in truth, and with a perfect heart, and have done that which is good in thy sight. This Sermon God made useful to me; and after this, it pleased the Lord to order it so, that I changed my condition, and the Lord provided for me a good Husband, one that feared him. And some troubles being here: many of the people of God went for *New England,* and among them my Husband desired to go, but I and my friends were very averse unto it. I, having one childe, and being big with another, thought it to be very difficult to cross the Seas with two small children, some of my Neighbors advising me to the contrary, living so well as I did. But I told them that what the Lord would have me to do, that I would willingly do; and then it pleased the Lord to bring that Scripture to my mind, *Eph.* 5. 22. *Wives submit your selves unto your own Husbands, as unto the Lord.* And then my heart was brought off to a quiet submission.

Ro2

But after this, I being well delivered, and the Child well; It pleased the Lord soon after to take my Child to himself: Now upon this, so far as it pleased the Lord to help a poor wretch, I begged earnestly of him, to know why he took away my Child, and it was given in to me, that it was because I would not go to *New England*. Upon this the Lord took away all fears from my pirit, and then I told my Husband I was willing to go with him. For the Lord had made my way clear to me against any that should oppose. And then my husband went presently upon the work to fit to go. And the Lord was pleased to carry us as upon Eagles wings, according to that *Deut.* 32. 10, 11. We were eight weeks in our passage, and saw nothing but the Heavens and Waters. I knew that the Lord was a great God upon the shore: But when I was upon the Sea, I did then see more of his glorious power then ever I had done before, according to that of the Psalmist, *Psal.* 107. 23, 24. And when the Lord was pleased to bring us in safety on shore, his people gave us the

the best entertainment they could, and then
I thought I could never be thankful enough
to the Lord for his goodness in preserving
us upon the Sea, I being big with Childe,
and my Husband sick almost all the Voy-
age. After this my Husband would have
gone by water higher into the Countrey.
But I told him, the Lord having been so
good in bringing us safe ashore amongst his
people, I was not willing to go again to
Sea. And it was a good Providence of
God we did not, for most of them that
went were undone by it. The first Sermon
that I heard after I came ashore was out of
*Jer. 2.13. For my people have committed two
evils; They have forsaken me the Fountain of
living waters, and hewed them out Cisterns,
broken Cisterns that can hold no water.* Now
the Minister did shew, that whatever we
did build on short of Christ, would prove
but a broken Cistern; and by that Sermon
the Lord was pleased to shake my foundation: but I being a poor ignorant creature,
thought if I could but get into the fellowship of the People of God, that that would
quiet my spirit, and answer all my Objecti-

D ons

ons ; And I did accordingly attempt to joyn
with the Church; but they were very faithful to the Lord, and my foul, and asked me
what Promise the Lord had made home in
Power upon me. And *I* answered them,
Jer. 31. 3. *Yea, I have loved thee with an everlasting love, therefore with' loving kindness I
have drawn thee.* But they told me that that
was a general Promise ; that I must look to
get some particular Promise made home in
Power upon me, and perswaded me to wait
a little longer to see what God would further do for my poor foul, which accordingly
I did. And going to hear Mr. *Cotton,* who
did preach out of *Rev.* 2. 28. *To him that o-
vercometh I will give the Morning-star,* from
which words he did observe, that that Star
was Chrift. And this he came to shew, how
a foul might know whether it had an inter-
eftin Chrift or no, and that was by the
Lords giving out such precious Promises as
these to the poor foul, *viz.* That God was
in Chrift reconciling the world to himself,
2 *Cor.* 5. 19. and that John 16. 23. *And your
joy shall no man take from you.* And *Ifa.* 54.
22. *I have blotted out as a thick cloud thy
trans-*

tranfgreffions, and as a cloud thy fins : and that
Ifa: 43- 5. which Promifes afterwards God
made fweet to my foul. After this I went
to hear Mr. *Shepherd,* and he was preaching out of the Parable of the ten Virgins;
Matth. 25. 1. 13, I, his difcourfe he fhewed
that all were Profeffors, but the foolifh had
nothing, but Lamps without oyle, a Profeffion without grace in their hearts : but
that the wife had got grace in their hearts,
and fo were ready prepared to meet the
Bridegroom when he came. Now, by that
difcourfe of his the Lord was pleafed to
convince me that I was a foolifh Virgin and
that I made a Profeffion, but wanted the
oyle of grace in my heart, and by this means
I was brought into a very fad condition;
For I did not experimentally know what it
was to have oyle in my Lamp, grace in my
heart, nor what it was to have union with
Chrift, that being a myftery to me: And
then I did think my felf guilty of breaking
all the Commandments of God except the
fixth. For I thought I had neither defired,
wifhed or endeavoured any mans death. But
then the Lord fhewed me, That if I were

D 2   faved

faved by Chrift, my fins had murdered him,
according to that *Acts* 3.15. *chap.* 4.10. And
that did greatly aggravate my fin the more
unto me. Now one of my Neighbors ob-
ferving that I was in a diftreffed condition,
told me that fhe had been a hearing, and
that the Minifter fhe heard was a fhewing,
that the Lord had more glory in the falvation then in the damnation of finners. For
in their falvation, his Mercy and his Juftice
were both glorified, but in their deftruction only his Juftice was glorified. Hearing
of this, the Lord was pleafed to draw out
my heart to plead with him, That if he
might receive more glory in my falvation
then in my deftruction, that then his Mercy
might be manifefted to me. For I thought,
although I had many worldly comforts, yet
I had no intereft in Chrift, and that if I
fhould die prefently, Hell would be my portion ; and in this fad and fore diftrefs, the
Lord was pleafed to imprint that Scripture
upon my mind, *Job* 10.2. *I will fay unto God
do not condemn me, fhew me wherefore thou con-
tendeft with me* ? *Job* 40.2. *Shall be that con-
tendeth with the Almighty, inftruct him* ? *He
that*

that reproveth God, let him answer it; and that word of the Apostle, *Rom. 9.20,21: Nay, but thou, O man, who art thou that repliest against God. Shall the thing formed say to him that formed it, Why hast thou made me thus? Hath not the Potter power over the clay, of the same lump to make one vessel unto honour, and another unto dishonour.* After this, it pleased God, that Mr. *Elliott,* and some other of the people of God, seeing me in this sad condition, told me the Church would have me come in to be a Member with them; but I did reply, that all Church-fellowship would do me no good. Then Mr. *Elliott* asked me, What would do me good? and I told him, Nothing but an interest in Christ. His Answer was, That I was already in the pangs of the New Birth; and he did believe it would not be long before the Lord spoke peace to my poor soul. After that, reading a book of Dr. *Prestons,* where he did shew, *that when the Lord joined himself to a believer, he did first comprehend the soul, and then enabling the soul by faith to apprehend him.* Which double Act of faith I then knew not. About fourteen days after, considering what a distressed condition I was in, I was bemoaning my self before the Lord; and the Lord was pleased to bring that Scripture to my remembrance in *John 16. I will give you that joy, that no man taketh from you.*

And then I thought with my self that it was Christ that I did want, and not joy: But the Lord brought that Scripture to me, *that Christ was tidings of great joy. Luke 2. 10, 11.* And I thought how could this be to such a poor wretch as I was, and the Lord was pleased to bring that Scripture to my mind, *That he looked not as man looked, 1 Sam. 16 7.* And that he was God and not man, *Hos 11. 9* And by this means he took away all my fears. And then the Lord did help me to discern that this was a mystery indeed, and did so quiet my heart, that all the World seemed as nothing unto me. For I never heard such a voice before, blessed be his Name.

And then the people of God would have me come into fellowship with them. And soon after I was admitted a Babe in Christ among them. Afterwards, being

to

to hear Mr. *Gatten*, on 1 Pet 2.2. *As new-born Babes desire the sincere milk of the words, that you may grow thereby.* And from thence he shewed, that if it were a living Babe it would cry out for nourishment, and that that soul that did once really taste of Christ was never satisfied, but would still be crying out for more and more of Christ; when such a soul came to any Ordinance, as Hearing, Prayer, the Lords Supper, and did get nothing of Christ, they were all as lost Ordinances to it.

It so fell out, that the next Lords day was the day of sitting down at the Lords Table. And the Lord did put it into my thoughts, that if we received nothing but a piece of bread and a sip of wine, it would be but a poor empty thing; and so the Lord did help me to beg, that if what he had been pleased to speak to my soul before were a true manifestation of himself that he would be pleased to speak again unto my soul. For a three-fold cord is not easily broken, *Eccles.* 4. 12.

D 4 Being

Being at the Ordinance, the bread and wine coming about, I was thus sighing unto the Lord, what shall I have nothing but a bit of bread and a sip of wine this day? And the Lord was pleased to bring that Scripture to my minde, *John* 6. 55. *For my flesh is meat indeed, and my blood is drink indeed.* And so the Lord was pleased to give something more of himself to my poor soul at that time. After this, a sad Providence attended one of my Neighbors, I was full of fears that her condition might be mine. But the Lord brought that Scripture to my mind, *Jer.* 29. 11. *For I know the thoughts that I think towards you, saith the Lord, thoughts of Peace and not of evil, to give you an expected end.* And thereby the Lord stayd my heart in trusting upon himself, and giving me a safe delivery. And being up again, I went to hear Mr. *Cotton,* and he was shewing what Assurance was and how happy that soul was that could say as *Job* did, *Job* 19. 25. And with *David, Psal.* 119. *For ever Lord thy Word is setled in the Heavens ;* and so the Lord was pleased to shew me what a mercy I had that had Assurance, Then I went to speak to

Mr.

Mr. *Cotten*, to ask him what he thought of the work of God upon my poor soul. And he told me, that he was satisfied that it was a real work of God. And he did counce me to walk humbly and thankfully, and to take heed of grieving that Spirit of God by which I was sealed up to the day of Redemption, and to walk humbly towards those that God had not revealed so much of himself to as he had to me. And then the Lord was pleased by his Providence to call my Husband to come for *England*, and he did tell me, that he should so order business that I should have less of the world to trouble me; I was glad to hear it from him, and desired him to go. And then the Lord was pleased to help me to consider whether I had not got a better Husband; and the Lord did quiet my heart in himself, my soul being espoused to him, 2 *Cor.* 11. 2. After he was gone from me, we did hear of a War broke forth in *England*, and friends told me my Husband would be in danger of his life if taken. I told them the best I knew, and the worst I knew; and that if God should take my Husband out of the world, I should have

a Husband in Heaven, which was best of all.
And Mr. *John Elliott* did visit me in his absence, and asked me how the Lord did bear
up my heart in my Husbands absence. And
I did tell him, that the Lord was as well able
to bring him to me in safety, as he did to carry him out. And he answered me, I believe
the Lord will say unto thee as he did to the
Canaanitish woman, *Matth.*15 28. Be it unto thee according to thy faith. And the Lord
was pleased to keep me and all that I had,
and to preserve him, and to bring him home
in safety unto me. And then in stead of having less of the world which I desired, the
Lord did cast in more of it. After this, my
Husband told me, That he must go again to
England, and I was very unwilling to it, but
he told me, if he did not the Name of God
would suffer. To prevent which, I consented, and it pleased God to bring him home
in safety to me. And in a few years after, he brought me over to *England* and
God shewed much of his goodness to
me.

At my coming ashore, he brought that
Scripture to my Remembrance *Deut.*33.
26, 27.

26, 27. *There is none like unto thee, O God of Jshurun, who rideth upon the Heaven in thy Help, and in his Excellency on the Sky, the Eternal God is thy Refuge, and underneath are the everlasting armes.*

After it had pleased God to bring me back to my Native Countrey. I was much troubled that there was no better observation of the Lords day, it being our Practice in *New-England* to begin it at Sunne-set the Evening before, as it is Recorded in *Genesis, That the Evening and the Morning was the first day;* and that Scripture was brought to my Memory, *Prov.* 14. 10. *The heart knows its own bitternesse, but no man intermeddles with its joy:* Many trials the Lord hath been pleased to exercise me with, but in the midst of all God hath made that Word sweet to my soul, *Isa.* 54. 10. For the Mountains shall depart and the Hills be removed, but my kindness shall not depart from thee, neither shall the Covenant of my Peace be removed, saith the Lord that hath mercy on thee.

It

It pleased the Lord after a year or two to exercise me with much weaknels; but then he made that Word fweet unto me, *Ifa 50.8. He is near that juftifies me, who will contend with me.* And that word, *Job 15. 11. Are the confolations of God fmall unto thee?* After thefe things, when *I* was in a very great ftrait, upon the apprehenfion of fome publick dangers that feem'd to threaten us, the Lord was pleafed to bring to my mind that Scripture, *Zach. 9.12. Turn to your ftrong Holds you Prifoners of Hope.* And fince in the midft of my many bodily infirmities God hath made that word fweet to my foul, *Pfal. 116. 7. Return unto thy reft, O my foul, for the Lord hath dealt beautifully with thee.* And that word, *Pfal. 23.4. Though I walk through the valley of the fhadow of death, I will fear no evil, for thou art with me, thy rod and thy ftaffe they comfort me.* I will remain as a prifoner of hope, waiting for a fruition of that happinefs which the Lord Jefus Chrift hath prepared for me. *For I know he that hath the Son hath life. 1 Iohn 5.12. And if the Son make us free, then are we free indeed, Iohn 8.36.* And bleffed is that people that knows the joyful found, they

fhall

shall walk, O Lord, in the light of thy countenance. I finde the Lord Jesus very free in
the tenders of his love to poor sinners. And
that love hath in a great measure been manifested to my poor soul. After this it pleased the Lord to visit one of my Daughters
with a great sickness, upon which my heart
was drawn out to seek the Lord on her be-
half, then that Scripture was brought to my
mind, *John* 11. 21. *Then said Martha unto
Jesus, Lord, if thou hadst been here, my Brother
had not died. But I know that now whatever
thou wilt ask of God, God will give it to thee.
Jesus saith unto her, thy Brother shall rise again.
Martha saith unto him, I know that he shall rise
again at the last day. Jesus saith unto her, I am
the Resurrection and the Life, and he that believes in me shall never die.* And it pleased
the Lord to give me her life at an Answer of
Prayer. It pleased the Lord after this to visit this Land with the Pestilence, a severe
stroak of his, that swept away many thousands; and under that sad Providence of his
the Lord did help me to rely alone upon himself, from that Scripture, *Psal.* 91. 7. *A thousand shall fall at thy side, and ten thousand at
thy*

thy right hand, but it shall not come nigh thee. And according to my faith, it pleased the Lord to preserve both my self and all my Relations from that sad stroke, though some of them were often in the midst of danger, blessed be his Name. The next year after the Lord did again (for our sins) visit us, and that by a dreadful fire, which reduced to ashes many thousand houses, and yet his love was then manifested to me in the preservation of my habitation, when many better than my self were burnt out. Therefore unto my God shall I, (who am less then the least of all his mercies) render that praise which is due unto his Name.

Since that, whilst I was upon a languishing bed, and Death even knocking at the door, it pleased the Lord once again to alarme me in that weak condition by a dreadful fire which brake out very near us, and at that time it pleased my good God to support and strengthen my spirit with that Scripture, *Isa.* 43. 2. *When thou passest through the waters, I will be with thee: and through the Rivers, they shall not overflow thee: when thou walkest through the fire thou shalt*

not

not be burnt, neither shall the flame kindle upon thee. And that Scripture, *Isa 54.5 For thy Maker is thy Husband, the Lord of Hosts is his Name, and thy Redeemer the Holy One of Israel, the God of the whole Earth shall he be called.* And this second time also the Lord was gratiously pleased to preserve me and my House from that amazing stroke which did so much threaten us; And O that all these new and old Experiences might be high obligations upon me and mine to holiness and fruitfulness all our days.

Whilst I remained in *New-England* there hapned a great Earthquake which did shake all in the house, and my son being by me, asked me what it was, I told him, our Neighbours were all amazed at it, and knew not but that the world might then be at an end, and did run up and down very much affrighted at it, but I sate still, and did think with my self what a Christ was worth to my poor soul at that time. And then God made these Scriptures sweet refreshings, supporting and quieting my soul.

Psal. 18. 46. *The Lord Liveth, and blessed be my Rock, and let the God of my Salvation be exalted*

Heb.

Heb. 11.13. *These all died in faith not hav-*
ing received the Promises, but having seen
them afar off, and were perswaded of them, and
embraced them, and confessed they were stran-
gers and pilgrims on the earth.

Rev. 7.9. *After this I beheld, and lo a great*
multitude, which no man could number, of all
Nations, and Kindred, and People, and Tongues,
stood before the Throne and before the Lamb
cloathed with white Robes and Palmes in their
hands, ver. 14. *And he said to me, these are they*
which came out of great tribulation, and have
washed their Robes, and made them white in the
blood of the Lamb.

FINIS.

Bridges Remains, being Eight Sermons; viz. 1. Of
Mans Blessednesse, &c. By Mr. *Bridges* Preacher
of the Word of God at *Yarmouth.*
A Discourse of Christs Coming. By *Theophilus Gale.*
The Nature and Principles of Love, as the End of the
Commandment, declar'd in some of the last Sermons
of Mr. Joseph Caryl, with an Epistle of Dr. Owen D.D.
All to be sold by John Hancock Sen. and Jun. at the
Three Bibles in *Cornhill.*

The Mothers Blessing (Wing M2937) is reproduced by permission of The British Library, Shelfmark C142dd3. The text block measures 66 × 117 mm, A4.

C 142 dd 3

64

5 AP 58

The Mothers Blessing;

BEING

Several Godly Admonitions Given
by a Mother unto her Children
upon her Death-bed, a little before her departure.

Printed for F. Coles, T. Vere, J. Wright,
and J. Clarke.

A N

HVNDRED

GODLY LESSONS.

THe Materials and ingredients, of
which our bodies are composed, do
declare unto us that they are mortal, and subject unto Death, which dictate
of Nature, old Age like a true and infalli-
ble scribe hath (as you my Children may behold) long since written on my furrow-
ed face; and besides now at this time,
sickness, which is deaths harbinger, and
immediate fore-runner, hath cast me on my
weary couch, and by denying me the least
cast of rest, declares plainly, and makes
me sensible, that the time of my departure

is at hand : Yet ere I leave the world, as
Parents are wont to bestow Legacies, and
to settle their estates upon their heirs, so
do I, your declining Mother confer that
which I have, upon you, my obedient children. Much wealth I have not, therefore
I cannot leave you rich, for I was never
any of Fortunes Darlings ; loaded with a-
bundance. And it is my wish in this matter concerning you : that as I have not hitherto greedily coveted, or covetously affec-
ted the goods of this world, so neither any of
you for that time that you have to live in
this miserable world, be either too studious
or solicitous in desiring or procuring the
fading and perishing treasures of this Life :
thus having begun to tell you what I would
have you for to shun, I proceed further to
tell you still what I would have you to a-
void ; take heed of all manner of sin, flie
from it as from a Serpent ; let not the world
entice, nor the flesh allure you unto vanity,
and as I would not have you wrong your
selves by sinful acts, so neither would I have
you to be injurious unto others ; remember
that old saying of which I have made so oft
times mention : Do unto others as you
desire theirs should do to you, and what you
would

would not have others do to you that do
not you to them. By remembring and constant meditating this, you shall not miscar-
ry in your actions. Thus having heard
what you shall shun, now learn what
you are to follow, piety towards God: and
awful respect, and reverence unto all those
Magistrates whom he hath plac'd in authority under himself, and love and charity to
their inferiours. For your duties towards
God. Open not your Chamber Doors before you have opened Heaven by your prayers; let your prayers be the key to open the
Morning and also the bolt that shuts up the
night, 'tis this that in time of want must
furnish you with all those things which you
stand in need of; yet this is not enough to
pray unto him for blessings, unless ye
praise him for those blessings which you
have received, and hereby you shall shew
your selves thankful, and silently invite new
blessings to be poured upon you, be obedient to his commands, let this sacred word
be a light unto your feet, and a lanthorn unto your paths, and desire his blessed spirit to
steer your course through the Waves of
this world, and you shall be sure to arrive
safely at the Haven of Happiness.   Perad-

A 3   it

The Mothers Blessing : Or,

the Magistrate, which I would have you outwardly to expres by an awful respecting, and reverencing of their persons and authority. Lastly, towards your inferiours, carry your selves mildly and gently. But because Songs and rhimes may make a better impression, and stick faster in your memories, hear them in verse.

———————————————

G AP 58

F I N I S.

———————————————

An *Hundred* Devout Admonitions left by a Dying mother to her children.

Being moſt neceſſary and Excellent Directions for a Religious and Chriſtians converſation.

AN

A N

Hundred godly Leſſons.

My children dear mark well my words,
　　and keep my Precepts well,
Conſider daily in your minds
　　the words which I ſhall tell :
The gain is great which ſhall enſue,
　　good counſel doth direct,
Their ways and actions for the beſt,
　　that do it not neglect.

Firſt Worſhip God above all things,
　　vain Swearing ſee you ſhun :
Hear much, but ſee you little ſay,
　　thereby much good is won ;
Speak thou no ill of any man,
　　tend well thine own affairs,
Bridle thy wrath and anger ſo,
　　that thereof come no cares.

B2

Be mild and gentle in thy speech,
 both unto Man and Child,
Refuse not good and lawful gains,
 with words be not beguil'd :
Forget not any good turn done,
 and help thy Neighbours need,
Commit no ill in any case,
 the hungry see thou feed.

Cast no man in the teeth with that
 which thou for him hast done ;
Remember flesh is fond and frail,
 and hatred see thou shun.
Leave wicked things, then no mishap
 shall thee to trouble bring,
Crave no preferment of the Lord,
 nor honour of the King.

Boast not thy self before God's sight,
 who knows thy heart alway :
Offend not thou the multitude,
 faint not when thou dost pray :
Scorn not a man in misery,
 esteem not tatling tales,
Consider reason is exil'd,
 when as a Drunkard rails :

           Use

Use not thy lips to loathsom lyes,
   by craft increase not wealth,
And strive not with a mighty man,
   with temperance nourish health;
Look that thou order well thy words,
   leave not thy friend for gold;
Trust not too much before thou try,
   in venturing be not bold.

In God repose thy strength and stay,
   with tongue extol his praise:
Honour thy Parents, and the Lord
   he will prolong thy dayes:
He that his Father honour doth,
   God will forgive his sin;
He that his Mother loves, is like
   one that doth favour win.

A child obedient to the Lord,
   his Mother comfort shall,
The Fathers blessing stays the house,
   his curse doth make it fall:
A wise child makes the Father glad,
   Fools do their Mothers grieve:
And shame shall come to such as do
   their Parents not relieve.

He that his Mother doth defie,
   shall come to naught and worse,
The Ravens shall pick out their eyes,
   that do their Parents curse :
From needy men turn not thy face,
   let not thy right hand know,
What thou dost with thy left hand give,
   or on the poor bestow.

They that upon the poor bestow,
   unto the Lord do lend,
And God unto such men again,
   a thousand fold will send :
As water doth the fire quench,
   whose fury great doth grow,
Even so shall mercy quench their sins,
   the which do mercy show.

Hear thou God's word with earnest care,
   with wisdom answer make,
Be thou not mov'd with every wind,
   such course do sinners take ;
Thy talk will shew thy fame or shame,
   fools oft themselves annoy,
Trust not thy own will overmuch,
   for that may thee destroy.

Thou

They that the living God do fear,
  a faithful friend shall find :
A true friend is a jewel rare,
  and comfort to the mind.
Hear Sermons that good sentences
  thou maist conceive aright,
In Gods commandments exercise,
  thy self both day and night.

Think on the pain thy mother had,
  in bringing thee to life ;
Fear God who knows thy secret thoughts,
  and look thou make no strife.
Visit the sick with carefulness,
  the Prisoners grief consider,
Shew pitty to the fatherless,
  and God will thee deliver.

Help still to right the widows wrong,
  remember still thine end,
So thou shalt never do amiss,
  nor wilfully offend :
Trust not a reconciled friend,
  more then an open foe,
Who toucheth pitch, shall be defil'd,
  take heed thou do not so.

                            Take

The Mother's Blessing : or,

Take not a wife that wanton is,
　　and full of shameful words,
The flattering of an horlot is,
　　at length more sharp then Swords.
Cast not thy love on such a one,
　　whose looks can thee allure,
In every face where beauty is.
　　the heart's not always pure.

A woman fair and undiscreet
　　is like a Ring of Gold,
The which in a swines snout is set,
　　unseemly to behold :
The malice of lewd women shun,
　　for they will thee destroy,
Hate her that doth on every man,
　　set her delight and joy.

From others let thy praise proceed,
　　boast not thy self in ought :
And do not hear a flattering tongue,
　　thereby much ill is wrought :
The child that doth his Parents rob,
　　and counteth it no sin,
A vile destroyer he is deem'd,
　　and shall no favour win.

Correction

An hundred godly Admonitions.

Correction bringeth wisdom sound,
    fools hate good counsel still,
That child doth shame his mother much,
    that's let to have his will
The good mans path shines as the light,
    that beautifies the day,
The wicked know not where they walk,
    for darknese is their way.

Put far from thee a froward Mouth,
    a slanderous tongue is ill,
And do not thou an envious mind,
    in any wise fulfill.
A Harlot brings a man to beg,
    in her is found no truth,
In gladness therefore live and dye,
    with the wife of thy youth.

Much babling breedeth great offence,
    he that speaks least is wise,
Gods blessing only makes men rich,
    from thence all ioys arise.
Better is little fearing God,
    then bags of gold got ill,
And better is one bit of bread,
    then a fat Ox with ill will.
        B

                          Who

Who brooks no warning hates his soul
    trurage is worship right,
A patient man far better is
    then one indued with might.
Mans credit comes by doing good,
    an humble mind indeed
Is better then a Lyar proud,
    from whence vain brags proceed.

By this dear children you may learn,
    how to direct your ways,
To God, to Prince, to Commonwealth,
    whereon your welfare stays.
Print well in your remembrance,
These Lessons I have sown,
    shall you live in happy state,
    when I am dead and gone.

FINIS.

These are the paths in which if you walk, you shall be happy: These are the streams that will convey you to the fountain of endless bliss and comfort, and by observing these precepts you shall surely live: but on the contrary, if you shall slight my speeches, and tread these precepts under-foot, you shall neither be happy here, nor

B2   bless

blest hereafter. But my breath now begins
to fail me, and inforceth me to be silent ;
Remember therefore these fore-going precepts, meditate daily on them, and I would
not have you think that to be enough only
to remember and to meditate, but to be sure
to practise them, so shall you all be happy in
this life, and eternally happy in that that is
to come, amiable shall you be in the sight of
Men and Angels, men shall respect you, the
Angels shall protect you, and the God of
Men and Angels shall crown you with joys
unspeakable, into which joys the Lord Jesus
receive my spirit. Amen.

A Wife Woman buildeth her Houfe, the foolifh deftroyeth it with her own hands.

Favour is deceitful, and beauty is Vanity: but a Woman that feareth the Lord, fhall be praifed.

She over-feeth the ways of her Houfhold: and eateth not the bread of idlenefs.

Her Children rife up and call her Bleffed: her Husband alfo fhall praife her.

AN untamed horse will be stubborn, and a Wanton Child will be wilful.

If thou bring up thy Son delicately, he shall make thee afraid, and if thou play with him, he shall bring thee to heaviness.

Laugh not with him, least thou be forry with him, and least thou gnash thy teeth in the end,

Give him no liberty in his youth, and wink not at his folly.

Bow down his neck while he is young, and beat him on the fide, while he is a Child, least he wax stubborn, and be disobedient unto thee, and so bring forrow to thine heart.

Chaftife thy Child, and be diligent there in, left his shame grieve thee.

5 AP 38

FINIS.

5 AP 58

John Pennyman's

INSTRUCTIONS

TO HIS

CHILDREN.

Which also may be of service unto o-
thers, and therefore they are thus
Published.

Reade in Fear, that you may receive a
Blessing.

LONDON,

Printed, and are to be given by the Author,
or to be had at *Dorman Newman's* Shop,
Bookseller, at the King's Arms in
the *Poultry,* 1674.

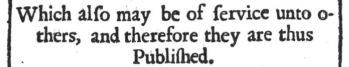

DEAR CHILDREN,

Hearken diligently to the Counsel and Advice of your Parents, for they watch over you for your good.

IN the *First* place, let the fear of the LORD, who is the searcher of your hearts, be alwayes in your minds, that in awe of Him, you may for ever stand ; not daring to bring the least Reproach upon His holy Name, by any Miscarriages of yours ; so shall you be CHILDREN to His praise, and a comfort and blessing to your Parents.

Secondly, See that none of you render evil for evil unto any one ; but do you ever follow that which is good, both amongst your selves, and towards all men.

Thirdly, Take heed of letting out your minds and affections to visible things ; for they perish in the using, and bring trouble, and sorrow, to all whose hearts are set thereon ; but let your minds always be retired inwards, that you may wait to feel that which is not of this world, nor esteemed by it ; but only esteemed by those who know the vertue and excellency of it, and who have been willing to part with all to purchase it ; it is the PEARL of greatest price ;

happy

happy are they that have found, or that yet shall find it.

Fourthly ; Take heed of entring into many words, when you are bid to do any business, either by your Parents, Masters, or other Superiours; but with all readiness of mind, see you obey all their lawful Commands with diligence and chearfulness.

Fifthly, Beware of mentioning the Name of the LORD in any case but with fear and reverence ; for His Name is Hallowed by them that fear Him, but taken in vain by those that fear Him not. And though they seem to Praise or Pray unto Him, yet such Services without His fear are an *Abomination* : wherefore take heed you be not deceived by those who are only in the good Words and fair Speeches ; but let your minds be kept single to the LORD, and He will shew you who they are that draw nigh to him with their lips, when their hearts are far from Him, and from such you are to turn away.

Sixthly, Let your words be few ; and be alwayes more ready to hear than speak, especially when the question is not asked you ; but when 'tis your place to speak, be sure it be in Mildness, Love and Gentleness ; lest through your provocation you cause others to sin, and then you will not be guiltless, for their sin will be charged upon you : wherefore let this be always

ways

ways in your remembrance, and for ever ob-
serv'd by you (as it hath been the practice and
experience of your Parents) to give mild and
soft answers ; for they do often turn away
wrath.

Seventhly, Whatever you see Vertuous in
any , be sure to follow that; and what you
see amiss in others, diligently search your own
hearts, lest your selves be found guilty thereof;
for it's an easie matter to see and find fault with
another (most can do that) but few love to examine themselves : be you (my dear CHIL-
DREN) of that number, lest you perish with
the multitude ; for the way is broad that leads
to destruction, and many walk therein : Therefore whilst you are young seek after true *Wisdom*, and it will guide and lead you in that narrow way, which all the holy Men walked in,
and in which all must walk, before they can enter into *Eternal Rest*.

Eighthly, Beware of reading foolish and vain
Books, which tend only to the corrupting of
Youth, and dishonoring the LORD ; Wherefore
heed you only those that tend to Holiness and
Vertue.

Ninthly, Consider how the LORD hath
blessed and prospered your Parents ; notwithstanding the fury and rage of our enemies, who
have accounted us as the greatest transgressors,
and judged us as the vilest of sinners ; and all

this

this for no other cause but only for the dif-
charge of our Consciences in the matters of
our GOD.

Tenthly, I warn you, as I did at the first,
so I do again charge you, that you walk in fear
and in humility all the dayes of your being
upon the Earth ; then shall you know that the
LORD hath not only blessed and prosper'd
your Parents, but will also bless and prosper
you : but if you depart from his fear, and cast
these my instructions behind your backs ; then
know, that you shall perish in your own iniquities, and I shall (thus far) be clear in my
conscience concerning you.

J. P.

DEAR CHILDREN,

*Since my writing the former Instructions, these
following came into my mind to impart unto you.*

1. BEware of a lying, flattering, deceitful
tongue ; also beware of Pride and high-
mindedness; and an exalted Spirit ; for such the
righteous GOD will judge.

2. But be you adorn'd with Faithfulness,
Meekness and Patience ; and let your behavi-
our be modest, courteous and gentle towards
all : and what-ever you would have others do
unto you, be sure you do that unto them ; and
heed

heed not so much theirs, as your own Duties.

3. Busie not your minds with others concerns; but be you careful and diligent in the discharge of your own; and then you need not be troubled what reproach you bear for them.

4. Bear patiently Afflictions, for they are good for you; therefore hasten not to be deliver'd from them; but in the retiredness of your minds consider the cause, and being better'd thereby, bless the LORD for His Mercies; *for whom He loves, He chastises.*

5. Be careful with whom you associate; and chuse none to be your intimates; but such who are exemplary in Vertue and Goodness: so will you avoid much contention and trouble.

6. Be ready to do good unto all as opportunity is offer'd; and take heed of wasting any of the good Creatures; for if you be unfaithful in those things that are earthly, who shall commit to you those that are heavenly.

7. Be not desirous of Riches or Honour; neither covet that which is anothers; but be content with your present conditions, and learn to be as well satisfied with want, as abundance; then will you follow the steps of your Parents, who have learned contentment what ever befals them.

8. Beware of jeering, or scoffing at any; neither give abusive or scurrilous language (either by Tongue or Pen by) for that will pro-

voke

voke the LORD's Anger againſt you, and bring reproach and trouble upon your Parents, who alwayes diſliked, yea abhorred ſuch things.

9. Be careful your hearts and minds be kept clean within, and then you need not be adviſed to have your words and actions clean without, for that will unavoidably follow.

10. Be not haſty in reproving or correcting of any ; but if (you live to be) call'd thereto, let it be in Love and in Wiſdom ; and if the offence be great, let it be with ſeverity, yet not in anger, or paſſion ; for that will harden them againſt you, and ſo inſtead of bettering them, you will thereby become tranſgreſſors your ſelves.

11. Beware that your wills bear not rule in any caſe ; but let Truth and Righteouſneſs alwaies be the ſway of your Judgments ; then will you be delivered from that great iniquity which hath ſo deeply corrupted many.

12. Be ſure you have regard to the oppreſſed; and take heed how you make advantage of anothers neceſſity, but rather conſider how you may be helpful unto them ; alwaies remembring the Parable of the good Samaritan, Luk. 10.33.

13. Be cautious for whom you are engaged, or unto whom you are oblig'd ; for ſuch things do often prove ſnares : but be more ready to give, then to receive ; and yet be ſure to acknowledge the leaſt kindneſs ; for ingratitude is hateful.   14. Be

14. Be not felf-ended; neither spend too much upon your own particulars, either in meats, drinks, clothing, or any thing elfe, for that may be a hindrance to the good you fhould do; but rather be fparing in that which relates to your felves, that you may be in the better capacity to do the good you ought to perform unto others.

15. Be not found in many needlefs words; neither contend with fuch as are in them, for that begets ftrife, but as they (out of the evil that's in their hearts) bring forth evil things; fo do you (out of the good that is in yours) bring forth good things.

16. Be not grafping after earthly concerns; for they bring trouble and forrow; and yet how many through their eager defires after fuch things, have choaked that good which once ftirred in them : wherefore take warning, and learn this as a truth experienc'd by me; that a little will fatisfie a contented mind.

17. Be not defirous after that knowledge, which will lift and puff up your minds; neither be too prying into thofe Myfteries that are hid ; but if the LORD fhould reveal any thing unto you , be fure of leave, when and to whom to impart it , not daring, either to add, or diminifh; for that has been (and is this day) a great and fore evil.

18. Beware of taking up your reft in any
outward

outward form of Worſhip, but keep in ſubjecti-
on to the fear of the LORD, who may lead into, or out of ſuch things as He pleaſeth; ſo let
him be your guide all your dayes, though you
ſhould be hated of all for His ſake; for our eyes
have ſeen the ſad fruits and effects of thoſe that
have gone about to ſet limits and bounds to His
Leadings.

19. Beware of imitating other mens words,
geſtures, or actions; that relate to religious performances; for *Imitators*, as well as *Image-ma-
kers*, in Worſhip, are an *Abomination*; and yet
thouſands do err and have erred herein : Neither be followers of the *vain Faſhions* & *Cuſtoms*
of this World; but whatſoever is *vertuous* and
of *good report*, that you may and ought to follow.

20. Be not haſty in judging other mens
Actions, wherein you have neither command
nor certainty; it being not barely the Action,
but the Spirit from whence it proceeds, that
makes it either accepted, or rejected : therefore
take heed leſt you condemn that, which GOD
juſtifies : for many are guilty herein, notwith-
ſtanding it's written, *Judge not according to outward appearance*; but if you do, you muſt as
well as they, witneſs *Sorrow*.

21. But leſt, through many words, your
minds ſhould be drawn forth, and (as but too
too many have been) hurt thereby; it's with
me

me to conclude, with thofe two great and weighty Commandments, *viz.* the firft is, *You fhall love the LORD with all your hearts, with all your fouls, and with all your ftrength.* And the fecond is like unto it, namely, *You fhall love your Neighbours as your felves :* for upon thefe two Commandments depend all that can be written, or fpoken, concerning your Duties either to GOD or Men.

J. P.

Hear me your Father, O Children, and do thereafter, that you may be fafe.

IF you come to ferve the L O R D, prepare your fouls for temptation. Set your hearts aright, and conftantly endure, and make not hafte in time of trouble.

Whatfoever is brought upon you, take chearfully : For, as Gold is tried in the Fire, fo are acceptable Men in the Furnace of Adverfity.

So incline your ears unto *Wifdom,* and apply your hearts to Underftanding , and feek her as Silver, and fearch for her as for hid Treafures : then fhall you underftand the Fear of the LORD , and find the Knowledge of GOD.

Happy is the man that findeth *Wifdom,* and the man that getteth Underftanding : But where is Wifdom to be found ?. and where is

the

the place of Understanding ? The Fear of the
L O R D, that is Wisdom ; and to depart from
evil, that is Understanding.

Wisdom exalteth her Children, and layeth
hold of them that seek her ; they that love her,
love life, and they that seek her early, shall be
filled with Joy ; and wheresoever she entereth,
the LORD will bless ; and if you commit your
selves unto her, you shall inherit her.

But at the first, she will walk with you by
crooked wayes, and bring fear and dread upon
you, and torment you with her discipline, until
she can trust your Souls, and try you by her
Laws.

Then will she return the streight way unto
you, and comfort you, and shew you of her secrets.

But if you go wrong, she will forsake you, and
give you over to your own ruine.

And when they cast up the accounts of their
Sins, they shall come with fear : and their own
iniquities shall convince them to their face.
Then shall the righteous man stand in great
boldness, before the face of such as afflicted
him, and made no account of his labours:
when they see it, they shall be troubled with
terrible fear, and shall be amazed at the strange-
ness of his Salvation, so far beyond all that
they

they looked for. And they repenting and groaning for anguish of Spirit, shall say within themselves, This was he whom we had sometime in derision and a proverb of reproach. *We fools counted his life madness*, and his end to be without honour. How is he numbred among the Children of GOD, and his lot among the Saints?

MY Dear Children, suffer not your minds to wander abroad, but heed your Fathers Counsel that it may be well with you, when our dayes are finished on earth, and we taken from you, or you from us; therefore ever follow that which draws your minds after holiness, and chuse that good part, which can never be taken from you; so shall you excel in all Vertues, and answer our greatest desires for you.

The riches and glory of this world I never sought for you, nor my self; but with carefulness have sought after an inheritance in that *Kingdom* which is not of this World, for that cannot fade away. Often hath my Soul been and is humbled before the LORD, to consider his manifold Mercies to us; Can it ever be forgotten how we were preserved in the late great *Plague* and *Fire!* and Trials much greater then those have I been carried through since; that I might

might be also proved in that which came nearest to me, and seemed the hardest.

Dear Children, I your Mother have tried many; and my love hath been in great sincerity to those in whom I found uprightness and simplicity, even to such was I made willing to give up my self as a Servant, for their honesties sake; and with them I walked in meekness and fear : but coming to be try'd whether my Soul could cleave to the LORD only, then some began to limit my Conscience to their apprehension and sight; this I durst not consent to; but my cry was in secret, concerning those, that would be as Lords there, *O you cruel Task-masters, will you not let me go to my Father ?* For my heart was fill'd with pantings and longings after the LORD, which constrain'd me to yeild obedience to what-ever I believed was His will, who had been to me a mighty Deliverer in many straits.

To bridle the liberty of the Spirit, is the greatest Tyranny in the world. Sharoon of Wisd. p. 244.

Children, in some part you have been witnesses how the love of my nearest friends (as well as others) have been turned into evil surmisings against me; and why was it ? but because I could not part with my integrity; but rather than so, gave cause to those, who judged by outward appearance, to take offence against me;

me; but in all thefe things I appeal to Him
who hath known the fecrets of my heart, and
hath feen the true tendernefs I have had towards thofe, who at the fame time have writ
and fpoke bitter things againft me. Whom have
I wronged, or defrauded? or againft whom hath
my tongue dared to fpeak lies? Not any that I
know of. So Children, truft you in the LORD
only, and not in mortal men; for they will
fail you when the *Crofs* comes to be taken up
to your and their wills: and though this is fet
down for your warning; yet affuredly my
love is to them all, and can fay to fuch, as
Jofeph did to his Brethren; *be not grieved with
your felves though you fold me hither,* (even under
great reproach) for we were to be feparated.

Dear Children, gather your minds inwards;
fear the LORD all your dayes, and you fhall receive His reward; which hath been great to
your dear Mother,

Mary Pennyman.

*This is my Commandment, That ye love one
another,* John 15. 12.

*Strive for the Truth unto Death, and de-
fend Juftice for your Lives: and the
LORD GOD will fight for you.*

THE END.

'An Appendix' from Anthony Walker, *The Holy Life of Mrs. Elizabeth Walker* (Wing W305) is reproduced, by permission, from the copy at the Folger Shakespeare Library. The text block measures 85 × 141 mm, page 81.

The text contains the following misnumberings. (The correct number appears in brackets.):

pp. 229 [213], 232 [216], 233 [217], 236 [220], 237 [221], 240 [224].

THE
HOLY LIFE

O F

Mrs Elizabeth Walker,

Late Wife of *A. W.* D. D. Rector
of *Fyfield in Essex.*

Giving a modest and short Account of her
Exemplary *PIETY* and *CHARITY.*

Published for the Glory of *God,* and provoking others to the like *Graces* and *Vertues.*

With some usefull PAPERS and LETTERS
writ by her on several Occasions.

*Chiefly designed to be given to her Friends,
who can abundantly testifie to the Truth of what is
here related.*

LONDON,

Printed by *J. Leake,* and are to be Sold by
Nathanael Ranew, at the *King's Arms*
in St. *Paul's Church-Yard,* MDCXC.

A N
APPENDIX:

Containing some few of the Directions she wrote for her Childrens Instruction, mentioned Sect. 12. *And some few Letters written by her.*

I Desire it may be remembred she wrote these, not for grown and experienced Christians, who might be fitter to instruct her than be assisted by her, much less with the least Prospect they should ever be published or seen by many Eyes; my own never saw them till hers were closed; but I hope may be useful for young ones and Beginners, and as such I recommend them to her Friends to communicate to their Children, if they think good, and have not given them better of their own; and therefore it is not just to measure her Abilities by the scantling of this Performance, but to consider the End to which it was designed, to suit the Capacities, and assist

O 3

the

the tender Minds of those for whom they were written, when I guess they might be about twelve, or fourteen years of Age ; for one of them died at sixteen ; and with this equitable Allowance I hope they may be very passable, if not commendable and usefull.

For *my* Dear Children, Mrs. Margaret *and* Elizabeth Walker.

IT is the duty of **Christians** to Pray fervently and frequently, with Faith, with Humility, with Sincerity, with Constancy, with watchfulness, in the Spirit, with Warmth and Life.

Prayer is a means whereby we give *Worship to God*, giving him the Glory of all his adorable Perfections.

Prayer is the *Soul's Motion* to God ; *Desire and Expectation are the Soul of Prayer.*

Prayer is a *knocking at the Door of God's Grace* and Mercy in Christ for all manner of Supplies you stand in need of.

Prayer is a *Wrestling with God* ; the Lord is willing to forgive, ready to hear and help, yet he delighteth to have his Strength tryed, *Gen.* 32. 24, 25.

The

The work of Prayer is not so much to lift up the *Hands*, and *Eyes*, and *Voice*, as to lift up the *Heart* and *Soul*.

In Prayer is required extensiveness and intensiveness of *Mind*, and *Heart*, with Importunity, which consisteth in a frequent renewing of our Suits to God, notwithstanding all discouragements, with a *patient* waiting for returns of Grace.

Prayer must be a *Premeditated Work*, as to the Sins to be confessed, the *Wants* expressed, the *Mercies* acknowledged ; but especially to have right apprehensions of the *Purity*, *Majesty*, *Immensity*, *All-sufficiency*, *Fidelity*, and *Bounty* of the Lord, to whom you Pray ; with Faith in his Promises and Providences, and his *Almightiness* to supply your Wants in the things of this Life, and the Life to come.

Be much with God in Secret Prayer, and let not the *fire* of the Spirit, and *Holy Zeal* be wanting in any Duty, which, in the Hearts of God's People send out *Holy Vapours* of fragrant spiritual Desires and Requests to God, *Vials full of Odours*, which are the *Prayers of the Saints*, Rev. 5. 8. compared to *sweet Incense*, Mal. 1, 11. How near are the Saints thus exercised to Jesus Christ ? There is but a *step*, as it were, between them and Heaven. What precious answers of Grace receive they oftentimes from the *Oracle* of God.

You

You will do well to obferve the fitteft *Seafon* for Secret Prayer; though a Chriftian is to Pray at *all times*, yet at *fometimes* more efpecially; when we meet with any *new Occurrence* of Providence, every frefh difpenfation of Providence is a *prompt* to Prayer, as when any *Affliction* befalls us, *Jam.* 5. 13.

So when any *frefh Mercy* is received, it is a fit feafon to go afide, and to acknowledge *God's Goodnefs*, and our *own Unworthinefs*, 2 *Sam.* 7. 18. When you find the Spirit of God *moving* upon your Soul, exciting you to the Duty, *Cant.* 2. 10. your Hearts fhould anfwer again, *Thy Face Lord will I feek*, *Pfal.* 27. 5.

When you find your Heart in a *fettled* and *compofed Frame*; then alfo is a fit feafon for fecret Prayer. When, as *David's*, *your Heart is fixed*, not difturbed with any Secular Bufinefs.

The *Morning* alfo is a fit Seafon for Secret Prayer, the Mind is moft compofed, and troubled with feweft Diverfions. (See her Practife, *Sect.* 5. *pag.* 33.

It were well to be with God as *foon as you awake*, to offer up to him the firft-Fruits of every Day; this was, with others, *David's* manner, *Pfal.* 5. 3. 139. 3.

The *Evening* alfo is a fit Seafon for Secret Prayer, *Pfal.* 55. 17. not only to begin, but to conclude the Day with God: Sleep not till you have begged his Pardon for your Sins committed,

mitted, and Praiſed him for the Mercies re-ceivedthat Day.

When you go about any *Holy Duty*, ſet by all Worldly Occaſions ; ſay to them as *Abraham* did to his Young-men, *Stay you here while I go aſide and Worſhip God*, Gen. 22. 5.

Do not ordinarily go to Prayer when your *Anger* is ſtirred, and your *Mind* full of *Perturbation*, 1 *Tim.* 2. 8. leſt you offer up the Sacrifice of a Fool, 1 *Kings* 19. 11, 12. and ſpeak unadviſedly with your Lips.

Do not actually engage in Prayer when you are inclined to *Sleep* and *Drowſineſs* ; you muſt be *wakefull* when you Pray, if you would *watch unto Prayer.*

Alſo allot, and ſet out a *due Proportion of Time* for the Duty of Prayer; a *ſlighty huddled Prayer is a blind Sacrifice ; carleſſneſs in Prayer, breedeth and feedeth Inconſtancy, and Inſtability in Prayer.*

Slightineſs in Prayer is an inlet to deluſive Fancies, and is a fore-runner of *Apoſtacy*, if not ſeaſonably reduced : Such Religious Performances go out like the *Snuff* of a Candle.

It is not enough to chuſe a *fit time*, but you muſt allow *ſufficient time* to Pray : If you are *ſtraitned* in your *Time*, you will be *ſtraitned* in your *Prayer.*

Alſo a great help in the well-performance of the Duty of Secret Prayer, is to take *Pains* with your Heart by *Meditation.*   A s

As the offering of *sweet Incense* was prepared and compounded of many *costly Materials*, *Exod.* 30. 34. so is a *Spiritual Prayer*, not *rudely* and *confusedly*, but *deliberately, advisedly, preparedly*, and very *particularly* presented before the Lord.

It is usually from *want of preparation* you find such *deadness* and *indisposedness* in Prayer; a heedfull and deliberate *reading* of the *Holy Scriptures* before Prayer, is also a great *help* for the well-performing of the Duty.

A farther help in the duty of Prayer, is to have *right conceptions of God*, conceive of him *as he is*, and as he hath *revealed* himself in his Word to be; an *Omnipresent* God, *Psal.* 139. that he is *really*, though not *visibly*, present in all Places, and in that Place where you are Praying; that he *sees* your *Heart*. Whenever you set about this, or any Holy Duty, *set God before your Eyes*, and represent him under the Notion of an *Omnipresent, all-seeing God*.

Conceive of God as one full of *Majesty* and *Greatness*, infinitely above any of his *Creatures*: This Apprehension may much both *quicken us*, and *awe* us in Prayer.

Conceive of God as one that is *exceeding Gracious*, and *Plenteous in Mercy* to all that call upon him.

To apprehend God in his *Greatness*, doth stir up *Fear* and *Godly Reverence*; to apprehend
God

God in his *Goodnefs*, doth ftir up *Faith* and *Holy Boldnefs*.

Conceive of God in Prayer as *one God*, not divided in *Effence*, yet diftinguifhed into *three Perfons*; the *Father*, the *Son*, and *Spirit*, all concurring to the Prayers of Believers, and have a different office about them ; there is the *Father Hearing*, the *Son Interceeding*, the *Spirit helping our Infirmities*.

Conceive of God not *abfolutely* but *in Chrift*. God in *himfelf is a confuming Fire*, Heb. 12. But *in Chrift* he is a *Mercifull Father* ; there is no coming *unto God but by Jefus Chrift*, Heb. 7. 25.

Entertain, and *maintain* very honourable Thoughts of the Duty of *Prayer it felf*, this will both *move* you to the Duty, and much *quicken* you in the Duty.

What the *Pfalmift* fays of the *City of God*, *Pfal.* 87. 3. that may be faid of the duty of Prayer, *Great and Glorious things are fpoken of it*.

You may read of wonderfull effects of **Faith;** the *effects* and *fruits* of *Prayer* are as **many and** great. *Heb.* 11. It hath *obtained Promifes*, *fubdued Kingdoms*, *turned away Enemies* ; it hath *raifed the Dead*, *ftopp'd the Sun's Courfe*; yea *made it go back* ; it hath *opened Prifon-Doors*, and *unlocked Secrets* ; it hath *opened Heaven*, and *fhut* it again, with much Reverence be it
fpoken ;

spoken ; it hath *laid hold upon God himself*, and put him to a mercifull Retreat, when he hath been marching in Anger against *Persons or People*. God speaks as if his Hands were held and tied up by Prayer : *Let me go*, saith he to *Jacob* ; and, *Let me alone*, saith he to *Moses* ; as if the Lord would indent with *Moses*, and offer him a Composition to hold his Peace, *Exod.* 32. 10.

Wonderfull is that passage, *Isa.* 45. 11. if read right, God says, *Concerning the Works of my Hands command ye me.*

The *prevalency* of fervent Prayer is very great, it *prevails much* with God, *Jam.* 5. 15, 16. Keep your Hearts *close* to the duty, and suffer them not to *stray or wander*, a *straying* Heart must needs be a *straitned* Heart in Prayer.

If you would have your Heart *enlivened*, and *enlarged* in Prayer, remember to *repell* every *vain Thought* that comes in to your disturbance; *resist it*, and *call* in *help* from Heaven against it.

Let the *guilt* of no *one Sin* lie upon your *Conscience*, that will *clog*, *disquiet*, and *check* your Spirit in Prayer.

It is not amiss to observe a *method* in Prayer, especially when you Pray with others, (as she would sometimes do, when both my self and Curate were absent, rather than Family-Worship should be wholly omitted) though not

tyed

tyed to Words, but *confused Repetitions* and *disorderly Digressions* dif-affect those that join with you.

(*Though some prophane Scorners may mock and snear at this, what real Evil scorn-worthy is there in it, for a serious, holy Mother to instruct her Daughters aforehand, to Pray with their Maids and Children, if God had spared them, and given them those Relations ? I wish no Mothers would give their Children Counsels or Examples more liable to Exception.*)

Chuse such a *Place* to Pray in as is most convenient, where you may not be disturbed by *noise in your Ears*, nor be *diverted by any Object before your Eyes* ; *shut also the Door* left the Wind of *Vain-glory* get in thereat. *Mat. 6. 5, 6.*

Be much in the use of *Ejaculatory* Prayer, which is a *short*, yet *serious*, lifting up the Soul in desires to *God. Gen.* 43. 14, 49. 18. *Neh.* 2. 4. 2 *Sam.* 15. 31. *Luk.* 23. 42. *John* 12. 27.

Ejaculatory Prayer is a special means to keep our Hearts very *Spiritual* and *Savoury* when often in Heaven ; it is a special means to fit them for more *solemn* and *continued* Prayer.

You may find this way of Praying very *familiar* with the *best* of Men ; yea, with *Christ* himself.

Al.

Also remember to set their *Examples* before your Eyes, who have performed the Duty of Prayer, with *life-enlargement* and *importunity.* See *Gen.* 32. 24. *Matth.* 26. 26.ᵉ39. *Heb.* 5. 7. *Hos.* 12. 3. *Examples sway us sometimes more than any Rules or Precepts.*

For farther Encouragement to this Duty of Prayer, consult with many other Promises: That of our Saviour's, where he saith, *Matth.* 21. 22. *Whatever you ask in prayer, believing, you shall receive.* And in *John* 14. 13, 14. *Whatsoever you shall ask in my Name I will doe it. If ye shall ask any thing in my Name I will doe it.* And *Matth.* 7. 7, 8. *Ask, and it shall be given you : seek, and ye shall find: knock, and it shall be opened unto you. For every one that asketh, receiveth: and he that seeketh, findeth : and to him that knocketh, it shall be opened.*

Call upon me, and I will answer thee; and shew thee great and mighty things, which thou knowest not, Jer. 33. 3.

Jam. 5. 15. *The prayer of faith shall save the sick, and the Lord shall raise him up ; and if he hath committed sins , they shall be forgiven him.——The effectual fervent prayer of a righteous man availeth much.*

Whosoever shall call upon the Name of the Lord shall be saved, Rom. 10. 3.

If any man want Wisdom, let him ask of God,
who

who giveth to all men liberally and upbraideth not,
and it shall be given him. But let him ask in
faith, nothing wavering; for he that wavereth
is like a wave of the Sea, driven with the Wind,
and tossed.

Thus she concludes, it may seem somewhat
abruptly, I can give no reason, and will not
guess; only the unwritten Paper which remains may seem to imply, she designed more.
This is just the *fortyeth* part of what she had
written for her Childrens use, being 6 *Pages*
in her Book, of *Twelve score*; so that I have
enough, if I would enlarge, to *tire* my self,
and *satisfie*, not to say, clog, my Readers. But
I will consult my own ease, and theirs, in adding little more of what an account is given,
Sect. 12. under Eleven or Twelve distinct
Heads.

I confess, I am tempted to add the *Example*
to the *Rule*, I mean the *large Form* of *Prayer*
and *Thanksgiving*, each containing 16 *Pages*.
But I'll forbear, only as I toucht a few Lines
of the beginning and end of the Thanksgiving
before.

So I shall give a little taste of this Prayer
which she begins thus.

'Good Lord, give me to *know* thee, who
'passest all *Knowledge*, and though I cannot
'*comprehend* thee in the perfection and full-
'ness of thy Glory, yet vouchsafe to give me
'to

' to apprehend thee, in thy *Love* and *pardoning*
' *Mercy* to me a poor miserable Sinner ; who
' in my first Being was invested with an *happy*
' and *righteous* Estate, from which, O *Lord,*
' in my *first Original,* I soon declined, &c. And
so proceeds most humbly to acknowledge the
guilt and pollution of Original Sin, as I *think,*
yea *know,* most *Orthodoxly.* If our *Bibles,* our
Articles, our *Homilies,* yea our *Liturgy,* be
more Orthodox than *Socinus,* and those *Ephra-
mites* who *lisp* his *Sibboleth,* because they cannot, or will not, pronounce aright the *Shib-
boleth* of the *Church of England*'s good old Doctrine.

Then she proceeds to a large Confession of
actual Sin, both of *Omission* and *Commission* a-
gainst *both* Tables. Acknowledging the deme-
rit of them, proceeds to sue out the Pardon of
them in these words.

' O God, thou knowest my foolishness, and
' my Sins are not hid from thee, I beseech
' thee pardon my Iniquities, and blot out my
' Transgressions, though they be as a *thick*
' *Cloud.* Good Lord, *wash me from my Impu-*
' *rities* in that *Fountain set open for Sin and for*
' *Uncleanness,* the precious Blood of Jesus Christ
' which is not only able to expiate my *guilt,*
' but to cleanse me from all my *filthiness,* that
' through *his stripes I may be healed,* and clean-
' sed from all my *Original* and *Actual* Defile-
ments,

ments, &c. Having enlarged upon this, she proceeds to pay for *Sanctification* and *Inherent Righteousness*, that she may be a *new Creature in Christ Jesus* ; then most fully and earnestly against *Temptation* ; then for the *Assistance of the Spirit* to render all God's Ordinances, and the means of Grace effectual ; then for *growth in Grace* ; for *Comfort* ; for an *Heavenly frame of Heart* and *Life* ; for *assurance* and manifestation of God's Love to her ; then for *Wisdom* to consider her latter End, and to be helped in that *Spiritual Arithmetick, so to number her Days as to apply her Heart to true Wisdom* ; then that God would *fit and prepare* her for her *Dissolution*, that when her days shall be consummated on Earth, her *Corruptible* may *put on Incorruption*, and her *Mortal put on Immortality.* Then she concludes with these Words:

Then shall *Death*, my *last Enemy*, be vanquished and *swallowed up in Victory*; and from thy unworthy Creature Everlasting Praises shall be rendred unto thee, through Jesus Christ that giveth me the *Victory*, for thou hast *redeemed my Soul from the Power of the Grave*. I beseech thee receive me into thy Eternal Kingdom and Glory, that *neither Death nor Life, things present, nor things to come may be able to separate me from thy Love, O God, which is in Christ Jesus my Lord.*

Then

Then she proceeds to Pray for the *Church*, of which a taste was given in her *Monday-morning Prayers*, *Sect.* 7. *pag.* 45. ' Gracious Lord, the ' Mercies I ask of thee for my own Soul, I ear- ' nestly beg of thee for thy Church and Peo- ' ple. Blessed Lord, *Thou hast made the Earth by thy Power, established the World by thy Wisdom, and stretched out the Heavens by thy Discretion*; *thy Arm is not shortned that thou canst not Save.* Good Lord take care of *Zion, build up the Walls of* Jerusalem, that in *Zion there may be Deliverance,* and Holiness in thy House ; let the *Mountain of thy House be established in the top of the Mountains* ; be thou a *Wall of Fire round about,* and *her Glory in the midst thereof,* ———But I forgot my self, 'tis hard to stop my Pen. Then, I beseech thee especially for the *Land* of my *Nativity,* the Nation of which I am a sinfull Member, --- here is a large Paragraph. The next is for the *World* ; Give thy Gospel a free and glorious Passage through the *World.* Good Lord pity those that sit in the *region and shaddow of Death.* --- Then, I beseech thee be mercifull to all the Sons and Daughters of *Sorrow, and Affliction,*--- the *Disconsolate,* the *Sick,* those who contend with *Poverty, Imprisonment, Reproach, Disgrace.* --- Then for them who suffer *Persecution for the Truth :* Then for her Relations. I confess, I am almost ashamed that I have thus mangled so ex-

cellent

cellent a Prayer, fo *Piously*, fo *Judiciously*, in
fuch *fuitable Scripture Phrafe* and Language.
I think it had been better to have tran-
fcribed the whole, or let it quite alone ; but her
Friends may command a Copy of it if they
pleafe. Having finifhed her Interceffions for
others, fhe returns to conclude with renewed
Petitions for herfelf, which I will venture to
fet down.

Good Lord, be the God and Portion of me
thy unworthy Creature, and of thofe fo dear
unto me ; give me a *Relation* to thee, an *Affi-
ance* in thee, and a *Dependance* upon thee, that
in all my *concerns* I may come to thee, in whom
are all my frefh Springs, the riches of free Grace
to poor Sinners, and treafuries of Mercies, purchafed with the Precious Blood of Jefus Chrift.
I befeech thee with-hold not thy tender Mercies from me, but give me of that *hidden Man-
na,* the fweet refrefhing Incomes of thy Holy
Spirit into my Soul, and when my Heart is
overwhelmed, I befeech thee lead me to the
Rock that is higher than I , for thou haft been
a fhelter to me. Lord be thou a *ftrong Tower to
me, to which I may continually refort ; for whom
have I in Heaven but thee ?* And if I know any
thing of my own Heart, *there is none* compara-
tive on Earth *that I defire befides thee ;* thou art
my God, *befides thee there is no Saviour.* I befeech thee *guide me with thy Counfel,* and when

I fhall

I shall go hence and be no more in this World I beseech thee *receive me into thy Glory*.

Then follows the *Thanksgiving*, full as large as the Form of Prayer, and, if it may be, more *Spiritual, raised*, and *Divinely Savoury* ; but I will not repeat the Errour, to mangle it, and set down so Imperfect Pieces, and spoil its Beauty, but signifie to her Friends, that I shall freely allow them to read the Original, which is fairly legible, or if they think it worth the while, to Copy it out, or at more leisure to Print some few Copies of it , and others of her usefull Papers, if desired ; which I omit at present for fear of swelling this into too great a Bulk, though I am sure several of them equal, or rather exceed any thing I have now Published of hers.

Marks

MARKS

OF A

Regenerate Estate.

I add this because it is concise, and will not take up much Room or Time. Giving her Children Directions how to examine and try the Estate of their Souls towards God.

D O you consent to the *Law* of God, that it is *true*, and *Righteous*?

Have you perceived your self *Sentenced* to Death by it ; being condemned and convinced of your natural, undone Condition?

Have you seen the *utter Insufficiency* of every Creature, either to be in its *self* your *Happiness*, or the *means* of curing this your *Misery*, and making you *happy* again in God?

Have you been *convinced* that your *Happiness* is only in God as the *End*, and in *Christ* as the *way* to him, and the *End* also, as he is *one* with

P 3   the

the Father; and perceivest thou that thou must be brought to God by Christ, or Eternally Perish?

Have you seen hereupon an absolute *necessity* of your enjoying Christ, and the full *sufficiency* that is in him to do for you whatsoever your Condition requireth, by reason of the *fullness* of his *Satisfaction*, the *greatness* of his *Power*, and *Dignity* of his *Person*, and the *freeness* and *Indefiniteness* of his Promises?

Have you discovered the excellency of this Pearl to be worth the selling all to buy it?

Hath this been joined with some *Sensibility*, as the *Conviction* of a Man that *thirsteth*, of the worth of *Drink*; and not been only a change in *Opinion*, produced by *Reading*, or *Education*, as a bare *notion* in the Understanding?

Is there an *abhorring* of all *Sin*, though your *Flesh* do tempt you to it?

Have both your *Sin* and *Misery* been a Burthen to your Soul, and if you could not *weep*, yet could you heartily *groan* under the unsupportable *weight* of both?

Have you renounced the *hidden* and *unfruitful works of Darkness*, having no *fellowship* with them, but with *Courage* and *Zeal* for God *reprove* them?

Do you labour to be *Holy* in all parts of your *Conversation*, watching over your ways at all times, and in all Companies?

Do

Do you make *Conscience* of the *least* of God's Commands as well as the *greatest*, avoiding idle Words, and vain Jesting ; abhorring all reproachfull Speeches, as well as violent Actions ?

Do you *love*, and *esteem*, and *labour* for the powerfull Preaching of the Word above all Earthly Treasures ?

Do you *Honour* and highly *account* of the *truly Godly*, and delight in the Company of such as sincerely fear God above all others, esteeming them the *excellent of the Earth* ?

Are you *carefull* of the *Sanctification* of the Sabbath, neither daring to *violate* that Holy Rest by Labour, nor to *neglect* the Holy Duties belonging to God's Service, publick or private ?

Do you not love the *World*, neither the *things* of the World, but heartily *desire* and *love* the things that concern a better Life, and so do in some measure *love the Appearance of Jesus Christ* ?

Can you *forgive your Enemies*, are you *easily entreated*, desirous of Peace, and to do good to them that *despitefully use you* ?

Do you set up a daily course of serving God, and that with your Family too, if you have any ; and renouncing your own *Righteousness*, trust only to the *Merits* of Jesus Christ ?

Have

Have you turned all your *Idols* out of your Heart, fo that the *Creature* hath no more the *Sovereignty*, but is now a *Servant* to God, and Jefus Chrift?

Do you *accept* of Chrift as your only Saviour, and expect your *Juftification*, *Recovery*, and *Everlafting Happinefs* from him alone?

Do you alfo *take him for your Lord* and *King*, and are his *Laws* the moft powerfull *Commanders* of your Life and Soul?

Do his Laws prevail againft the Commands of the *Flefh*, of *Satan*, and the *greateft* on Earth that fhall *countermand*?

And againft the greateft *Intereft* of your *Credit*, *Profit*, *Pleafure* or *Life*, fo that your *Confcience*, *Soul*, *Body*, *Life*, is directly *fubject* to Chrift alone?

Hath he the *Higheft Room* in your Heart, and Affections, fo that though you cannot love him as you *would*, yet nothing elfe is *loved fo much*?

Have you made an Hearty Covenant with him, and delivered up your felf accordingly to him, to be his for Ever without Referve?

Do you take your felf for *his* and not your *own*; is it your utmoft *Care*, and watchfull *Endeavour* that you may be found *faithfull* in his Covenant; and though you *fall into Sin*, you would not *renounce your Bargain*, nor change

your

your *Lord*, nor give up your felf to any other *Government* for all the World?

And if this be truly your *Cafe*, you are one of *God's Children* and *People*, and as *fure* as God's Promifes are *true*, there is an *happy* and *bleffed Eftate* for you; only fee that you abide in Chrift, and continue to the End, *for if any draw back, his Soul will have no pleafure in them*. Then fhe concludes with the Prayer fet down above, *page* 81.

For